I WANT
TO BE A
TEACHER

TESTIMONIES

A timely and inspiring book that challenges you to rethink the purpose of teaching. It is very important because Cathine Scott's personal life mirrors the principles she advocates.
—Dollie R. Robert, G & H Educational Associates, Inc.

A must-read book for anyone who wants to make teaching fun, fulfilling, and financially rewarding.
—Dr. Robert L. Scott, Real Estate Executive

I Want to Be a Teacher is simply one of the best books I have read about what it takes to become an outstanding teacher. It should be required reading for future teachers and anyone who is thinking about teaching.
—Ms. Dorothy Jones Kornegay, Retired Executive Assistant

This book is about the aspirations of the author and her colleagues. It tells us what it is to be a teacher and to love teaching and children. It will be read with interest and enjoyment by those in teacher education and by those who might want to know what teachers must know, must do, and should care about in general.
—Dr. Gertrude Henry, Retired Educator

Dr. Cathine G. Scott, educator, motivator, inspirer, and encourager, has contributed to teacher education and the teacher education programs where she worked.

—Ms. Giena C. Gilchrist, Business Executive

This book confirms my earliest impressions of Cathine Garner Gilchrist Scott as an outstanding teacher, a great expositor whose writing is not only clear, but a delight to read, and a lady with strong opinions, ideas, and solutions to problems, many of which she expresses very eloquently in this book ... It is deeply personal and wonderfully written.

—Ms. Rosetta Johnson, Professor of Business Administration

To sum up this book, it is one of the best books that I have read about an educator who inspires, motivates, and encourages others.

—Ms. Gretchen C. Gilchrist, Esquire

This book is truly a unique book which no one but Cathine G. Scott could have written. I think that all future teachers should read it.

—Mrs. Glenda Gilchrist-Pinkett, Educator

This book is a must-read for every prospective, current or former teacher. The conversational tone of the book makes it also a quick read ... so important in today's world. While the book will surely appeal to anyone interested or involved in teaching, it will also captivate readers from the general population, regardless of occupation or area of training.

—Louvenia Magee, Educator in the Prince
George's County school system

This book inspires others to want to be a teacher.

—Edward Garner, Jr., Esquire

I WANT
TO BE A
TEACHER

An Auto-Teachography in Three Parts:
Student, Professor, and Administrator

Cathine G. Scott, Ph.D.

Archway Publishing books may be ordered through booksellers or by contacting:

Archway Publishing
1663 Liberty Drive
Bloomington, IN 47403
www.archwaypublishing.com
1 (888) 242-5904

Because of the dynamic nature of the Internet, any web addresses or
links contained in this book may have changed since publication and
may no longer be valid. The views expressed in this work are solely those
of the author and do not necessarily reflect the views of the publisher,
and the publisher hereby disclaims any responsibility for them.

Any people depicted in stock imagery provided by Thinkstock are
models, and such images are being used for illustrative purposes only.
Certain stock imagery © Thinkstock.

ISBN: 978-1-4808-2623-6 (sc)
ISBN: 978-1-4808-2622-9 (hc)
ISBN: 978-1-4808-2624-3 (e)

Library of Congress Control Number: 2016903060

Print information available on the last page.

Archway Publishing rev. date: 6/5/2017

DEDICATION

To: Gretchen Cathine Gilchrist, Glenda Cathine Gilchrist-Pinkett, Giena Cathine Gilchrist (daughters), Louise and Edward Garner, (parents, both deceased), Leslie Smith Cobb (aunt) and Nevada Garner Jones (aunt, deceased) who, without knowing it, made me what I am today.

To: Dr. Robert L. Scott, my husband, for his support and encouragement while editing the book.

CONTENTS

FOREWORD

If you ever thought that you wanted to be a teacher, now is the time. The population is increasing, and there is a shortage of outstanding teachers in mathematics, science, and reading at the elementary and middle school levels. The American society needs the brightest and best teachers possible to inform, persuade, entertain, encourage, inspire, and motivate students to want to learn and become teachers. In today's competitive world, outstanding students who have the knowledge, skills, and dispositions to be effective in the classroom will be successful in obtaining the teaching positions they seek.

Cathine Garner Gilchrist Scott and I have been colleagues and friends for more than twenty-five years. We met when she came to the education department at Hampton University. We have worked together on education committees, discussed teaching ideas, and shared philosophies. When I first learned she was going to write this book, *I Want to Be a Teacher*, I did not know what to expect. Then after I read her draft and remembered some of our early discussions on education and our students, I knew she had much to share with future teachers.

Cathine has gone about her education career by trying to help students, current teachers, and future teachers as well. She understands the need for good teachers in our schools at all levels. As she describes her early education and the people who influenced her in the field, the reader may see many similar experiences and hopefully understand the real purpose of her story and her need to share. Many may have stories to share with others, but only a few shares them so that they will inspire others to be good teachers. In *I Want to Be a Teacher*, you will find such stories.

So if you really want to teach, read this book to see how Dr. Cathine G. Scott became an outstanding teacher.

Dr. Gertrude Henry, Retired Educator
Hampton University
Hampton, Virginia

AUTHOR'S PREFACE

Why this book? Why a full-scale discussion and presentation of *I Want to Be a Teacher.* More than twenty-thousand books may be published on education and teaching in the next two or more years. Why one more? Please permit me to tell you why I think that this is an excellent book for current and future teachers. I was teaching in the District of Columbia School District more than twenty years ago, and I became frustrated over the way some teachers were treating students, so I decided that I wanted to educate, develop, and train teachers. When I taught in several public school districts around the country, I received outstanding evaluations from the principals under whom I worked, and they informed me that I was an excellent teacher. I believed it. In fact, Ms. Alberta Beverly (deceased) and Dr. Herman Roebuck said that good teachers must have knowledge, skills, and a positive attitude and also must care about students. I had all of these characteristics, and I enjoyed imparting knowledge to students. I went to work at Hampton University, and I remained at the university for over 12 years. I continued as an educator for about thirty years, and then, I decided to retire. After I retired for three years, I concluded that future teachers should know about my life as a teacher and understand why I wanted to be a teacher. After reading Paul Halmos's book, *I Want to Be a Mathematician,* I thought that he had been a great teacher because he had inspired, motivated, and encouraged students to pursue mathematics. I thought to myself, *I have been inspiring, encouraging, and motivating young teachers to be great, so why not write about my educational career and experience. This will give other people who are thinking about becoming teachers an opportunity to know very early what it takes to be outstanding teachers.* Many teachers of yesterday would say that all teachers are expected to be competent, but not all teachers cared about students. Students who know that their teachers care about them will learn. In fact, in life, when the boss cares about the employees, the employees are much more productive and are willing to do more work for less money. So several years ago, I got the bright idea to write the book, *I Want to Be a Teacher.*

I think that current and future teachers should know and embrace the characteristics that are needed to be effective in the classroom. Future teachers thinking about the field of teacher preparation should have access to firsthand knowledge about what it takes to be great teachers.

So, if you have read this far, I am sure that you have an interest in becoming a great teacher. This book is great reading for any person who wants to pursue a degree in teacher education. It will give you insight into what and how you can be inspired to become a great teacher. It will also help you learn very quickly what you must know, do, and care about in order to be successful in today's classrooms.

The book is the story of my life as I moved from elementary school to the university level. It also focuses on my first job and how I went from obtaining a bachelor's of arts degree to a doctorate of philosophy degree. It progresses through the positions I held along the way as I continued to want to be a teacher. This book, *I Want to Be a Teacher,* came about because I am a passionate educator and world traveler who believes that good teachers belong in the classroom, and they need to know how to go from good to great to be effective in the classroom.

However, this book does have some views. It gives you only

my view of what it takes to be an empowering teacher in today's classroom. It does not teach you the knowledge and skills of a teacher preparation program, but it does show you that you need to know the foundations of a global education, understand curriculum, instructions, assessment, classroom management, and effectiveness.

This is an auto-teachography, an educational biography, about the career of a professional and passionate educator from the 1940s to now. It is presented more or less in chronologically order, moving from elementary school to the university level, to retirement, and then back to the university level. Its sections are organized by substance rather than time. It reveals my experience with the Diamond Grove Elementary School, the Edward W. Wyatt High School, and the colleges and universities I attended and worked. It expresses prejudices. It tells anecdotes, gossips about people, and preaches sermons. It discusses my time looking for a job, writing articles, writing a book, traveling, teaching, and editing.

What This Book Will Do for You

In every chapter of this book, you will find out what I did to achieve my dream of becoming a great teacher. You will find practical ideas, strategies, techniques, characteristics, and principles that will help you harness the tremendous power of becoming an effective teacher in today's classrooms. I believe that teachers are effective when the students learn. If teachers teach, but less than 50 percent of the students make passing grades, then the teachers have not taught at all. They think they have taught, but I think that they have not. So this book will show you how you can:

- become a great teacher;
- be successful in the classroom;
- encourage, motivate, and inspire students to be successful;

- help all children learn;
- plan, implement, and evaluate lessons;
- change your attitude to believe that all children can learn;
- use your mind for positive thinking about students;
- understand that you do not know everything;
- overcome the fear of teaching; and
- assess student learning in a positive way.

INTRODUCTION

My life as a nonfiction writer has led me to write this auto-tea-chography. After I read the research about autobiography and auto-ethnography, I coined the word *auto-teachography* to use to describe my personal experiences as a teacher. I concluded that the book could be a personal narrative similar to an ethnography, a biography, and a memoir in that it could examine qualities such as compassion, wisdom, mindfulness, creativity, self-awareness, and empathy. It could also include achievements of optimal health, well-being, and higher states of consciousness. It could include dream experiences, imitative experiences, revelations, life reviews, direct knowing, and creative inspirations (Pelias, 2003; Sparkes, 2000; and Allen, 2015). In other words, I say that an auto-teachography can draw on a form of autobiographical writing and an ethnography approach to research that describes and provides an analysis of personal experiences as a way to understand cultural experiences (Ellis, Adams, and Bochner, 2011). The auto-ethnography and autobiographical study may also be done in the form of memoirs, personal essays, short stories, journals, scripts, or poetry. It highlights actions, dialogues, emotions, spirituality, and self-consciousness. The writer's experiences are at the heart and core of the story (Varona, 2013; Wall, 2008; and Allen, 2015). In fact, Chang (2008) reported that some researchers have begun to challenge the status quo of traditional research by using personal narratives as rich primary sources to inform a study.

So by my definition, an auto-teachography is an educational biography written by its subject. It is definitely not an educational book or a book on teaching, and it is not the story of one's origins and life.

I am writing this auto-teachography because I want to share my knowledge and experiences with future teachers. Teachers must be well prepared to teach diverse students of the future. They need to know how to conduct research and access knowledge that may not be known already. They need to be critical thinkers, problem solvers, analytical and visionary thinkers, and transformational leaders for the future.

Future teachers should not learn just what is in the textbooks today. They need to think out of the box and realize that if they only know what is in the textbooks, their education will be out of date before they graduate from college (Halmos, P., 1985). Teachers need to be trained to solve problems, to be critical thinkers, to communicate effectively, to conduct research, and to collaborate with other teachers in their field.

Well, by now, you may ready know me. Maybe you know me as a college professor, a dean, a director, a faculty member, a sister, an aunt, a mother, or a wife, but do you really know me as a passionate educator? That is what being a teacher is—to be an educator and to be passionate about teaching.

I am Dr. Cathine Garner Gilchrist Scott, a writer, editor, teacher, consultant, and researcher. Writing this book took a lot of time. I started it more than five years ago, but I did not find the time to complete it until I retired as a dean of education. I wanted to write this book because I wanted future teachers to know what it meant to be a teacher. I was not sure that I could complete this book. I sought ghost writers, but I was not sure if they could tell the audience what I had in my mind. You will see that I taught elementary, junior high, high school, college, and graduate students. In short, I am glad that I wrote, *I Want To Be A Teacher.*

You can go to the archives in Emporia, Virginia and learn that my father worked as a civil engineer at the Rock Quarry in Skippers, Virginia for more than thirty years. I was the oldest of four children of the late Edward C. Garner and the late Louise Virginia Roberts Garner. My parents were not formally educated; therefore, I realized very early in life that I needed to go to college to be successful and to become a teacher. I attended the Diamond Grove Elementary School in Skippers, Virginia. It was a three-room school with desks for thirty students. The children who lived more than one mile from the school had to take the bus, while those who lived nearby walked. I lived too far from the school, so I rode the bus.

My mother, Louise, was very concerned about me going to school. We were very poor by today's standards, yet I did not know that I was poor. Mother made sure that I was clean and well-groomed each day. Her job was taking care of the four children. She made a nice lunch for me each day, combed my long red hair, and made sure that my shoes were clean and polished.

Each day my mother would tell me to do well in school. I had to remember that she had only gone to the seventh grade, and my father had never completed first grade. But every day, it was the same. She always told me to go to school and learn as much as I could.

My life as a teacher began when I was a little girl. I was always playing teacher and teaching the neighborhood kids mathematics. The neighborhood kids never wanted to do mathematics or reading. They thought that it was too hard, but I had a way of getting them to listen so that I could teach them. The neighborhood kids and I played all kinds of games using concrete objects, such as, counting bricks, sticks, and marbles. I would make up word problems and ask them to solve them. I would give word problems, such as, "If you have twenty-five cents, and you go to the grocery store to buy a soda and some candy that costs seventeen cents, how much money should the clerk give back to you?" However, many of them did not know that they were actually doing mathematics.

We played these kinds of games daily, and especially on the weekends when everyone visited each other.

Now, it is time for me to go to school. I turned six years of age in January, but I could not go to school until September. During that time, public schools did not have kindergarten programs in the rural towns of Virginia.

CHAPTER 1
STUDENT

Elementary School Years

In September 1947, I entered the first grade, already knowing that I wanted to be a teacher. My first grade teacher was Ms. Washington. I do not know her first name, but she was tall, slender, and very beautiful. I wanted to be like her. She taught me reading and arithmetic, as it was called then. She believed that if students could read, write, and compute, they could be successful. I never missed a day of school the entire year,  which meant that I was never ill or too sick to go to school. Ms. Washington would visit my mother, and they would talk about how well I was doing in school. Actually, I was the teacher's pet. In those days, teachers had special students to whom they gave lots of attention. In fact, the teachers liked the students who did well in school. Ms. Washington was always saying nice things to me and the other students. She seemed to have cared about the students.

The next year, September 1948, I was promoted to the second grade, and my teacher was Ms. Lois Hamlin. She was also a nice teacher and very beautiful. I liked her very much and wanted to be like her. When my birthday came in January, she had a birthday party for me. The party's spread consisted of crackers, yellow cheese, and punch. The students in the class sang happy birthday to me. I was so excited because I had never had a birthday party. I can remember Ms. Hamlin teaching me to read, write, and compute numbers. I remember her name because she and I have remained friends over the years. I was in contact with her until she left Raleigh, North Carolina. She said many times that she was so proud of me. She must have known that I had great potential for becoming a teacher. In fact, when I completed my Ph.D. in educational administration, she told me that she knew that I had great potential, but she never knew what opportunities that I would have. She was a young teacher when she came to the Diamond Grove School in Skippers, Virginia. The next year, she got married and moved to New York. I kept in contact with her even when I was in class with my third and fourth grade teacher, Ms. Edna Lee.

The next year, September 1949, I entered third grade. The third and fourth grades were conducted in the same classroom. Ms. Edna Lee taught reading and arithmetic. I liked arithmetic because I understood it, and I was eager to show her that I understood what she was teaching. I liked this teacher too. She was also tall, slender, and very pretty. She took me home with her one weekend, and I loved her from that day on. However, one day I did not understand a reading assignment, and she spanked me with a ruler. I disliked her for a very long time because I did not understand what she was asking of me. We remained in contact for more than twenty years until she passed away. I would visit her whenever I went home to see my parents. I told her that I wanted to be a teacher just like her. Of course, after she passed away, I forgave her, although she never knew that I was very angry with her.

I also spent my fourth grade year, September 1950, again with Ms. Lee. She taught us more reading and arithmetic. It seemed like we did the same arithmetic, except the numbers got bigger each year as I moved up the grades. She spent a lot of time using the old readers and other textbooks that were in the classroom. Although I liked Ms. Lee, I also disliked her. One morning I had not done my homework because we had no oil for the lamp, and my mother told me to tell the teacher that I could not read the assignment because we had no light. Well, I was so embarrassed to tell the teacher about the oil because I thought the other students might laugh at me, so I did not tell her or turn in my homework.

She tapped the hands of every student who had not completed the assignments. She tapped me very hard about five times. I cried and began to think that she did not like me anymore. Later on in the day when I had an opportunity to whisper to her why I did not do my homework, she said that she was very sorry. I was still very angry and disliked her because she had tapped me after all. I continued to do well in her class, but I did not like her anymore. I tolerated her because I knew that I had to do the work in order to get promoted to the next grade.

I spent fifth and sixth grades, September 1951 and 1952, in Ms. Warren's classroom. I do not remember her first name, but I do remember that when she became very angry with the students who did not know the answers to questions or who had not done their homework, she would throw the mathematics book on the floor. I often wondered why she became so angry with the students. Maybe she did not realize that those students who did not do their work or who did not know the answers to the questions never understood what she wanted them to do in the first place.

I continued to be a good student, and I studied mathematics more than any other subject. In fact, I can only remember studying mathematics and reading. I learned to read very well, and I enjoyed reading stories. Although I enjoyed reading, my parents never took me to the library. In fact, we did not have a car, so it was difficult to get to the library. We lived in the country, and we did not go places other than school, church on the first Sunday of each month, and maybe shopping sometimes on the Saturday prior to the first Sunday—that is, whenever we could get a ride with our neighbors.

Junior High School Years

I completed the fifth and sixth grades under Ms. Warren, and I was promoted to the seventh grade. By September 1952, a new school had been built for the black students in Greensville County, Virginia. The seventh grade students went to the new high school. It was named in honor of the late Edward W. Wyatt, an educator, who believed that all children should be educated. I entered the seventh grade in September 1953, and I went to the junior high section of the new school. There were three seventh grade teachers in the school. I met Ms. Edna Lee Hill again in the seventh grade. She had gotten married by that time. Ms. Evelyn Green and Mr. Lynch were the other two seventh grade teachers. Ms. Green and I became friends. She invited me to her house for a party with the neighborhood children. I liked her, so my parents found a way to get me to the party. She also knew that I wanted to be a teacher. I did not get to know Mr. Lynch very well. In fact, I never knew his first name.

In the seventh grade, we stayed in the same classroom all year, but the three seventh grade teachers must have known something about team teaching because the three classes met together to discuss social studies, and the three teachers rotated for mathematics, English, and science. In fact, Ms. Hill taught mathematics. Ms. Green taught English, and Mr. Lynch taught science.

The next year, September 1954, I was promoted to the eighth grade. We now were part of the junior high school. A good-looking, tall gentleman was our mathematics teacher, and I had a crush on him. I learned everything that he taught. He never knew that I did my mathematics because I liked him. If he is alive and reads my book, then he will know that he was responsible for me loving mathematics. I cannot remember any other eighth grade teachers. I am sure that I had English, science, social studies, and physical education, but somehow the names of those teachers escape me.

Senior High School Years

The next year, September 1955, I was promoted to the ninth grade. I remember the physical education teacher, the civics teacher, the Latin teacher, and my mathematics teacher. The physical education teacher taught us how to dress and how to match our clothes. She was a tall and slender lady. Her name was Ms. Young. During these times, students usually did not know the first name of teachers. I remember my Latin teacher, but I forgot her name. She was a very nice and kind person. She, too, was tall, and she dressed very pretty all of the time. She tried to help me to understand Latin, but I still disliked it because at that time, I did not understand its importance to understanding other words. However, I did well enough to pass the course. Today I know the importance of studying Latin.

The civics teacher was Mr. Ulysses Russell. He was short, fat, and light-skinned, and he was a very nice and friendly person. He was an excellent teacher by my standards today. He helped me to understand civics, especially when we talked about the governments of other countries of the world. He made the content interesting and exciting, and that excitement made me want to travel to some of those countries. During that time, I never knew that I would travel as much as I have traveled. In fact, I have traveled to every continent except Antarctica and Australia and to over 30 of the states of the United States.

The mathematics teacher was a tall and petite lady named Ms. Sledge. She later married and became Mrs. Adams. She was an excellent teacher by my standards today because she explained the concepts in such a way that I understood the content. I believe that when students understand what is taught, they will do well in class. By this time, I was taking algebra, and she helped me understand the subject. I have no idea where she is today, but I would like her to know that I like mathematics, and I teach it every opportunity that I have.

In September 1956, I was promoted to the tenth grade. I remember my English teacher, Ms. Newsome. I liked her, and she was a very nice and kind teacher. She caught me cheating one day on an English test when I was looking in the textbook for an answer. She did not call me out in front of the class. When she walked back into the classroom, she just said, "I saw that." I never cheated again in that class or any other time in life. I was too afraid of the consequences. I feared that I would get caught and would not like the results. I taught my children that they needed to study and not to cheat. They knew that if they cheated, there would be consequences, and I would not be able to help them.

I also remember my mathematics teacher who taught geometry, but I cannot recall her name. I remember that she was an older, light-skinned teacher with gray hair. I was considered one of the smart students in the geometry class. I liked geometry, but I did not like the teacher. She had her pets, but I was not one of them. Although I did well in her class, I would have done much better if I had liked her or felt that she liked me.

The physical education teacher remained the same, and she continued to make sure that we were physically fit, knew how to match clothes, and kept ourselves clean. I liked her, and I had an opportunity to play basketball. However, I never understood the game while I was in high school, and I did not appreciate and understand the sport until I went to college. In college, I attended many of the basketball games. Today, I like basketball and enjoy watching the games.

In September 1957, I entered the eleventh grade. I remember taking solid geometry. I had the same teacher as the year before when I was introduced to plane geometry. Now in a small high school, one teacher may teach all of the mathematics courses. I did not like the way that she taught solid geometry. She tried to make us see three-dimensional shapes on two-dimensional paper, and I never did understand the concepts that she was teaching. I had a difficult time. I just did not understand what she was teaching. I often wondered why she never used concrete objects like boxes and other concrete objects to help us to understand geometry. I decided then that I wanted to teach mathematics to help students to understand these concepts. As you continue to read this book, you will see that I grew to like geometry, and it is actually my favorite subject. I have found that most teachers today do not like the subject, but I think that it is because they do not understand it. I believe that if students understand geometry, they will be able to understand other strands of mathematics.

In September 1958, I entered the twelfth grade, and I was ready to graduate in June 1959. I remember my mathematics teacher. Her name was Ms. Adams. I had already taken algebra 1 with her, and now I was also taking algebra 2 with her. She made mathematics exciting, but she, too, did not use any concrete objects to help the students understand the concepts. I understood the mathematics because I worked very hard plus I liked her, which gave me more incentive to learn. Some students in the class did not do well. She also taught a combination of algebra and geometry, and that bridge became one of my favorite subjects in mathematics. In class, I sat beside another student named Edward Webb (now deceased). He was smart, and he seemed to like mathematics too. He and I studied together, and he helped me to understand the subject.

During my senior year, I ran for the homecoming queen and won. I had always wanted to be a queen. In fact, I wanted to be the queen since I was in elementary school. During the elementary years, all of the minority elementary schools in the state of Virginia performed activities during the month of May, which was called May Day. All the historically black schools in Greensville County competed in the May Pole activities, where elementary school students dressed up very pretty and wrapped the May Pole. A May Pole activity was one where in the students wrap a pole with colorful paper or strings wearing fancy clothes. The students at the Diamond Grove Elementary School always participated in the May Pole activities. The May Day queen was selected by the teacher, and each school had a chance of winning. I thought that I should have been selected as queen from the Diamond Grove School, but Ms. Edna Lee did not select me. She selected my best friend, Dorothyine Hunt. She was a beautiful queen and wore a pretty white dress. I was happy for her, but at the same time, I was jealous when I was not selected. Dorothyine and I were friends, and she never knew that I was jealous. We remained friends, and we are still friends today, although we lead different lives.

During September 1958, when I ran for the homecoming queen, Mr. Russell, the civics teacher, helped me write my campaign speech. He showed me how to campaign for the position to get the students to vote for me. I won that year because the student body voted for me, and I was very excited about being the homecoming queen. The queen rode on a beautifully decorated float in the community parade.

I continued to do well in all of my subjects. I graduated in June 1959 from Edward W. Wyatt High School. I was in the upper 25 percent of my class. I was very excited, but I did not know what to do next. I knew that I wanted to go to college to become a teacher, but my family did not have the money to pay for my college education. I had done well, but not well enough to receive a scholarship. I decided that I would work for a year and then go to college. I went to Kingston, New York, where my aunt Nevada Garner Jones, my father's sister, was living. I got a job working in a laundry. After one week I realized that I could not do that kind of work, so I quit and went to work at the Kingston Hospital as a nurse's aide. I would have become a nurse, but the di-  rector of the nursing school at the Kingston Hospital would not admit me to the nursing program. She told me that I had not scored high enough on the admission's test to be admitted, but I could go to the nursing school in New York City. At this time, the Kingston Hospital had never admitted a black student nurse.

As I worked as a nurse's aide, I watched the student nurses and started doing many of the things that they did. I knew that I could do what they were doing if only I had an opportunity. Although I did not want to be a nurse, I knew that I needed to go to college in order to be successful in life. I had passed the nursing examination high enough to attend the Belleview Hospital Nursing School, a black nursing school in Harlem, New York. I did not want to go to New York City because I was afraid to live alone or stay with other students. I had lived a very sheltered life. I had lived with only other family members who seemed to care about me very much. Because I was afraid to leave my aunt, I decided not to go to the nursing school in New York City. I knew that I wanted to be a teacher, but to become a teacher; I needed to go to college. So I decided to work for that year to save enough money to go to college the next year.

I worked at the Kingston Hospital during the summer, but by September 1959, I had not yet saved enough money to go to college. I had high hopes of going to Virginia State College in Petersburg, Virginia because many of the students in my high school class were going either there or to Saint Paul's College in Lawrenceville, Virginia. Later in the summer of 1959, I wrote a letter to a longtime family friend and respected educator who had been a supervisor of teachers in Greenville County, named Ms. R. L. Stamps (now deceased). I informed her that I could not attend Virginia State College because of financial reasons. She immediately wrote me a letter and told me to try Norfolk State College in Norfolk, Virginia. I had never heard of Norfolk State College. Unfortunately I did not have enough money to go to any college that year. So I decided to continue working to save enough money for the next fall semester. I told my aunt that I wanted to be a teacher, and I was going to work and save my money so that I could go to Norfolk State College in September 1960.

CHAPTER 2
BACHELOR OF ARTS DEGREE

I entered Norfolk State College in September 1960, fulfilling the first step to becoming a teacher. My first year at Norfolk State College was very exciting. I met many new people. Some became dear friends, while others remained as college acquaintances. I came to Norfolk State College as the homecoming queen from my high school, thinking that I was very smart and pretty. But when I arrived on campus, I found that many girls had been the homecoming  queen of their high school. This told me quickly that I was not the only smart and pretty girl on the campus. It did not take me very long to realize that when all of the girls were very smart and pretty, no one was smarter or prettier than the other. After I settled down, I made many friends, who are still my friends today.

During the first year at Norfolk State College, I took the traditional courses with many of the freshmen students. I enrolled in a mathematics course that was a remedial course. Not knowing it was considered a remedial course, I did very well in the class. In fact, I enjoyed it very much, and I received an "A" in the course. By this time, I had learned that students had to study whether they liked the teacher or not. In the mathematics course, I wondered why the teacher taught in such an abstract way and only showed us how to solve one example and then gave us a problem-solving test. Although I understood the concepts, I thought that the teacher should have taught the information in a more concrete way. I decided then that I wanted to teach mathematics so that students could understand what was taught and solve problems.

I do not seem to remember my other teachers during the freshmen year. I talked very much about wanting to be a teacher. I did not know at the time that many of the women I met at Norfolk State College also wanted to be teachers. You see, in the early sixties, many women thought that they could only become teachers or nurses. However, I did meet a student who was majoring in physics, and she said that she wanted to be an engineer.

During my freshman year, I was living with a family and three other students. I did not like all the noise and music that the students made. I had grown up as the only girl among three boys, so my living conditions had always been rather quiet. I read a lot and played alone. In fact, I stayed around my mother most of the time. The lady whose house we lived in at Norfolk State was very nice. She talked to me because she noticed that I did not have adequate social skills to interrelate with the other students. I stayed with her for about four weeks, and then, I went to see the dean of women at the college. I explained to the dean that I wanted to move to a quieter place. She said that she understood that there were several students living in the house, and she would find me another place. In fact, she said that she had just the perfect place for me. She gave me the name of Ms. Leslie Smith. This lady's husband had recently passed away, and she and her fifteen-year-old daughter lived near the college. Ms. Smith had already registered with the dean of women so that she could house a student, but she wanted a rather quiet and studious one. Seemingly, I was the right student for this lady. That very same day, I went to Ms. Smith's house, which was about a block from where I had been living. She had not gotten home from school when I arrived. I knocked on the door, and her daughter answered the door. I introduced myself, and she introduced herself as Bootsie. She invited me in, and I waited for her mother to arrive. I explained why I had come to her house. She told me that I could stay and showed me my room. I was very excited as I waited for Ms. Smith to arrive. About 5:30 p.m., this tall, glamorous lady, who was very friendly and poised came home. Bootsie introduced me to her mother, and she told her that the dean of women from Norfolk State College had sent me as a possible student to live with them. Ms. Smith talked to me about the possibility of living with her, and she asked me when did I want to move in. I said, "Right now." She said that I needed to wait because she needed to talk with the landlord of my previous residence, Mrs. Annie Harris. I said okay, but I still went to Mrs. Harris' house, packed my bag, and moved to Ms. Smith's house that very day. She said, "Well, I can let you stay tonight, but I must talk to Mrs. Harris." Ms. Smith and Mrs. Harris talked, and of course, Mrs. Harris said okay. She already knew that I did not fit in with the students at her house. Ms. Smith was a very gracious and kind lady. She only charged me $30.00 a month for food. I helped to clean the house on Saturdays. She knew that I was very poor, but I had great potential. She took me in and claimed me as her adopted daughter, and she began to make me into a real teacher.

After I settled in at Ms. Smith's house, I focused on my freshmen year courses. I took the traditional freshman general education courses. College was very exciting, and the courses were not very difficult. I was on my way to becoming a teacher. At the end of my freshman year, I was an average student with a 2.5 grade point average. The next year I returned to Ms. Smith's house. She now went by Ms. Cobb because she had remarried over the summer.

My second year at Norfolk State College was very exciting. I had to determine how I was going to pay for college because my parents did not have enough money for my tuition. One day I was talking to someone in the business office, and he told me about the national defense loan. Prospective teachers could qualify for the national defense loan to use the money to pay for their college education. The exciting thing about the loan was that if the teachers taught in the public school systems around the United States, the loan could be forgiven—one year teaching meant one loan forgiven. That concept was good for me because I wanted to be a teacher anyway. I continued with the general education courses. I took algebra 1, algebra 2, geometry, and trigonometry. I took other courses, but I don't remember them anymore. They must have been courses that were required in the general education program. I cannot remember any of the teachers' names, but I do know that the teaching style for mathematics was very abstract. I did not like the way that most of the mathematics professors taught because I did not understand what they were teaching. I had to struggle through the mathematics courses. Now keep in mind, I had wanted to become a mathematics teacher. I did not realize that to do well in mathematics, I must spend much more time studying and solving mathematics problems.

I finished my sophomore year with a 2.7 grade point average. I found that I was an average student who had to study very hard. After the semester, I began to study very hard and stayed focused so that I could be successful. I had started out with a strong desire to be a mathematics teacher, but at the end of my sophomore year, I flunked calculus 1. In fact, I flunked calculus 1 twice. The chairperson of the department of mathematics held a conference with me. He said that he had noticed that I had taken calculus 1 twice and that I must not understand the subject matter. He said that if I did not understand calculus 1, I would not understand calculus 2 and 3. "Well," I said, "you are correct. I do not understand it." To this day, I still do not understand calculus. In fact, I have learned over time that many mathematics teachers or some college professors do not seem to understand it either. Later in life, I asked a mathematics professor at one of the colleges where I had worked to explain the concept of calculus to me. She said that she did not understand it either. She just used the formulas to help the students get through the course. All I knew at that time was that calculus was a branch of mathematics that dealt with time, motion, and space, and supposedly, these elements never ended and were considered infinite.

The chairperson of the mathematics department said that I had a good background to be an elementary school teacher because I already knew more mathematics than the other students in the school of education. He gave me the name of the chairperson of the education department, Dr. Bowman. I immediately went to his office and told him my story. He reviewed my transcript and saw that I was an average student. I had taken more courses in mathematics than were required of elementary education majors. He gladly accepted me into the department of education. He also told me that I could still teach mathematics at the elementary school level and that I would make an excellent teacher of mathematics because I had so much more knowledge of the subject already than the other education majors. Back then, elementary school students were not involved with calculus; however, today all levels of mathematics are taught at the elementary and middle school levels.

The second semester of my sophomore year, I began to take education courses. My first course was introduction to education, which focused on understanding the philosophical, historical, psychological, and sociological foundations of education. I found the course very exciting. The instructor was excited about teaching and was also concerned about the students. I learned how to develop my own philosophy of education, and I developed my philosophy of education, which I still use today. That basic philosophy is that I believe that all students can learn and will learn if they are taught based on their learning styles. The professor of the course made teaching seem so simple and easy. There are two teachers in particular who made teaching exciting—Mrs. Vera Wilson and Ms. Margaret Johnson (deceased). They were dedicated teachers who were willing to help me become an excellent teacher. I took other education courses, but I do not remember any of them. I took whatever was required, and I did a great job because I was excited about becoming a teacher. I also did very well academically and developed excellent social skills.

During my junior year, I began to take methods courses that focused on what to teach, how to teach, and how to assess student learning. I enjoyed the course in methods of teaching arithmetic for elementary school teachers under Dr. Goss. She was a brilliant professor. Her class was well organized, and I learned how to teach arithmetic. She required that we design long ranged plans, unit plans, lesson plans, and use many hands-on activities to teach mathematics. I never worried about charts or any concrete objects. Remember, I was living with Ms. Cobb, a fifth grade teacher, and she wanted to help me. Good teachers seem to want to help other prospective teachers become the best they can be. We worked on charts, created tests, and found concrete objects to teach lessons whenever the professor said that I had to make presentations. I always opted to teach the fifth grade because I could receive help from Ms. Cobb. As a matter of fact, her classroom was just as pretty and colorful as she was. I never had to buy paper, pens, markers, or anything else to prepare a lesson plan. She always had appropriate materials that I could use in her garage. She was always making charts and boards so that her own lessons were more exciting. We used her dining room table as an office to make charts or whatever we needed to teach a lesson. The professor did not know that I was getting help from an excellent fifth grade teacher. All she knew was that I always presented an excellent lesson. My charts and lesson presentations on mathematics were always viewed as excellent. I received an "A" in the course. My self-esteem improved, and I began to feel that I really knew elementary school mathematics. I was on my way to becoming an excellent teacher. I did well in the other classes, but mathematics was my favorite. I saved the arithmetic book, and to this day, it remains in my library. The mathematics had not changed, and I soon realized that mathematics was an international language. I knew that all educated people should have a basic understanding of the mathematics taught at the elementary and middle school levels.

During my junior year, in addition to studying to become a teacher, I pledged the Alpha Kappa Alpha Sorority (AKA). This group of young women was also studying to become teachers, and I knew most of them already because we were taking education classes together. The AKA ladies thought that they were smart. Although we were engaging in various community activities and displaying ourselves on the campus, we managed to keep our grade point average to at least a 2.5. Some of those ladies are still my friends today. The AKA line was relatively nice, but some of the sisters did not treat me very well. One of the students in charge of the sorority was in my mathematics class, and she would try to harass me by saying, "Cathine, you may be smart in the arithmetic class for teachers, but you are not smart in here." I paid no attention to her or the other ladies because I had already decided that my main goal was to be a teacher. Besides, if they harassed me more than I thought I could take, I would have reported it to the college administration. Anyway, I survived the semester with no problems.

During my senior year, I did student teaching at two levels. Level one was a second grade class, and level two was a sixth grade class. I thought this process was excellent, mostly because I had an opportunity to be exposed to more than one level of teaching. In addition, this process would help me to be much more prepared to teach when I graduated. Prospective teachers often did not know what grade they would teach upon obtaining their first teaching position. My second grade class was under Ms. Lucinda Smith, a short, slender, and beautiful lady who was also excited about teaching. She had been teaching for more than ten years, and she was very comfortable in the classroom. She used many teaching aides for everything that she taught. I observed her teaching style for one week. Then she asked me to teach spelling the next week. I was so excited, but I was also very nervous because I did not know what to do if I made an error. She knew I was very apprehensive, so she said that we could plan the lesson together. We sat down together and began writing lesson objectives. She asked me what I wanted the students to know at the end of the lesson. That question was an excellent guide for me. In answering her question, I wanted the students to know several things. For example, I wanted them to (1) pronounce the words correctly, (2) arrange the words in alphabetical order, (3) identify the meaning of the words, (4) write a sentence using the words, and (5) spell the words correctly. I did not realize it at the time, but we had just written behavioral objectives, even though I had not studied behavioral objectives as such. They were not called behavioral objectives when I was in college. I do not remember what they were called other than purpose and aim. Nevertheless, I learned quickly how to write objectives that could be measured and assessed. The next part of the lesson plan focused on the activities to teach the objectives. Ms. Smith asked me how I would go about teaching the students how to pronounce the words. I told her that I could do several things. First, I would display the words on a chart, show the students some pictures, and ask them to tell me what was happening in the picture. Maybe the students would know some of the words. Secondly, I would pronounce the words myself, ask the students to repeat after me, and give me sentences using the words. I would ask the students to find the words in the newspaper, magazines, or other books, write sentences from the newspaper, and share the sentences with their classmates. Each day I covered a different objective, and on Thursday, the students were given a spelling test. Those students who scored 80 percent or higher did not need to take the test again on Friday. Ms. Smith then asked, "How do you plan to assess whether the students achieved the objectives?" Of course, my response was that I would give them a quiz, check the sentences, check the words in alphabetical order, and ask the students to write sentences using the words. She told me that I would make a good teacher. I was not sure because I had not actually taught a lesson, only engaged in the planning process. Little did I know, however, that good planning would bring about good teaching.

After we finished making plans for the week, Ms. Smith told

me that teachers made errors all of the time. She said that if I encountered an error, I should just stop, correct the error, and continue teaching. Of course, I said great and continued with my next lesson. I chose mathematics because I knew that I could teach mathematics, and I did an outstanding job. I collected visual aids, such as blocks, bottle tops, and cutout animals, among other things, to make the lessons exciting. I made all kinds of teaching aids and charts that communicated a message to students about learning. That idea probably came from Ms. Cobb, who was always planning to make her classroom exciting.

I continued to teach the elementary school subjects, and at the end of two weeks, I had taken full charge of the class. My anxiety had disappeared, and I had begun to feel like I was successful. Ms. Smith said that I was a fast learner and would make an excellent teacher. She was the kind of teacher who believed that teachers were born rather than made. However, she also said that prospective teachers could be taught the subject matter and content, instructional skills, and assessment tasks, but it was very difficult to teach them to care about students. I had to smile whenever she said such statements. She built up my confidence, and when the supervising professor from Norfolk State came to observe me teaching, I had confidence that I would do an excellent job. Of course, I chose to teach mathematics because I felt competent in teaching it. I liked the subject, and it was part of the elementary school curriculum. Many of my education colleagues disliked mathematics because they thought it was difficult. In fact, some elementary school teachers today believe that mathematics is hard and do not like the subject. That idea may be attributed to the fact that many elementary school teachers do not have a broad background in mathematics or science. I was very excited about the fact that I received an "A" in my first student teaching experience. Students were required to participate in a second student-teaching experience at a different level and sometimes even at a different school. My second experience was under a sixth grade teacher at the same school. I cannot remember her last name, but her first name was Beverly. She was a tall lady and very beautiful, but she was not as warm, friendly, and helpful as Ms. Smith had been. In fact, she was very stern in her mannerism to me and to the students. She had total control of her class, and by my standards, she was a strong disciplinarian. The students obeyed her, and they never made any unnecessary noise or disruptions in the classroom. She kept the students very busy moving from one activity to the next. She raised her voice very often, so I began to suspect that the students were actually afraid of her. Nevertheless, they did their work and appeared to have been good students.

Seemingly in the middle 1960s, cooperating teachers did an excellent job of training student teachers. I observed this cooperating teacher for one week, and then, I requested to teach a mathematics lesson. She was so excited that I wanted to teach mathematics. In fact, I was the first student teacher that she had supervised who wanted to teach mathematics as the first lesson. She was very excited about my teaching ability and style, especially in mathematics and science. You see, mathematics is a tool to use in teaching science, and I enjoyed both subjects. Little did this cooperating teacher know that Ms. Leslie Cobb had been my mentor. There was not much difference between the mathematics at the fifth grade level and the sixth grade level, just larger numbers. Ms. Cobb made sure that my plans were well written and that my charts were designed correctly and pretty. Of course, I did an excellent job in teaching sixth grade students, and I received another "A" in student teaching. I thought to myself that I was now on my way to becoming an excellent teacher.

While I was doing my student teaching, representatives from various school systems around the United States came to Norfolk State College (which is now Norfolk State University), looking for African American teachers. I interviewed with the representative from the District of Columbia school system, and the representative told me that when I completed my degree, I should give her a call. Well, I had already gotten married by this time, and my husband was already in the military and stationed in Washington,

DC, so I was excited about the possibility of obtaining a teaching position in the DC area.

I graduated from Norfolk State College in January 1965. I received an "A" in student teaching, and my cooperating teacher and college supervisor told me that I would make an excellent teacher. By this time, I had been told many times that I was an outstanding teacher because my students were learning. I soon began to believe that I could teach. In fact, Ms. Cobb, Ms. Wilson, and Ms. Johnson, all mentors who had helped me along the way, continued to tell me that I should continue in school to get a master's degree. But going back to school was not my top priority at that time. I was excited about the possibility of going to work and earning some money. You see, I had grown up very poor, and money had always been limited. So I went to work as a teacher in the District of Columbia school system.

CHAPTER 3
MY FIRST TEACHING EXPERIENCE

Elementary School Teacher

During the spring of my senior year, I interviewed with the District of Columbia public school system. After the interview with the personnel director, she gave me her card and asked me to call her when I graduated and arrived in Washington, DC. Well, I did, and I land my first teaching position at the Nicholas Avenue Elementary School in Washington, DC, under  the leadership of Ms. Alberta Beverly, the principal. She was a very nice and helpful principal, but the second thing that she said to me after she spoke and greeted me was that good teachers know how to control the class, and she did not want to see students in her office. She also said that good teachers are critical thinkers, problem-solvers, communicate well, use hands-on activities to motivate students, and they dress like they are going to a professional office. Well, she did not know that I had already been groomed for a teaching position, so she was impressed by how well prepared I was.

My first class was a junior primary class. These students came from low-income families in the Washington, DC area. The students had done well, but not well enough to be promoted to first grade, so they ended up in a program between kindergarten and first grade, called junior primary. I decided to use my critical thinking ability and problem-solving skills to do something innovative and very different from what the students had done in the past. I went to the classroom, rearranged the desks so that the students could work in groups, and begin to use many concrete objects and hands-on activities to teach reading and mathematics. I thought that if the students could learn to read and to understand mathematics, they would be on their way to success. In order to understand mathematics, students had to also know how to read. So reading was a top priority for me. The supervisor of new teachers in the DC school system visited new teachers on a weekly basis. The thinking was that the teachers needed to be observed first to determine where they needed help. Then, the supervisors could provide professional development where needed. The supervisor who came to see me was Ms. Glickenhaus, a nice German lady, with a strong accent. She observed me one time and told me that she wanted me to demonstrate how to teach reading for other teachers. Well, I was in my first year right out of college, and this was my first teaching position. I did not know that I had done such an outstanding job of teaching reading until she asked me to conduct a demonstration lesson for the other teachers. These other teachers had been teaching longer than a year, so I was not sure that I could show them how to do an effective job of teaching reading. On the other hand, mathematics was my specialty. I asked her, "How is a new teacher just out of college going to show veteran teachers how to teach anything? "Well," she said, "you have the potential to be an outstanding teacher, and I want the other teachers to see how you plan, organize, use concrete objects, move from one activity to the next, and bring closure to your lessons." I just thought that I was just using the normal teaching strategies.

Of course, I agreed to demonstrate the lesson, but I was so

nervous. I had only been in the school for one month, and I had not gotten to know all of the teachers or my students very well. I talked to another teacher who was also new to the school. This new teacher was Ms. Bernice Mack, a kindergarten teacher, who had been teaching for a long time in another school district. Her husband was in the military, and the family had moved to the Washington, DC, area. We became good friends, and we remain friends to this day. She was a tall, beautiful, slender, and fashionable lady who made her own clothes. She became my mentor. She taught kindergarten, and I taught the junior primary. I told her that Ms. Glickenhaus had asked me to conduct a demonstration for the other first grade teachers on how to teach reading effectively. I told her that I was so nervous. She told me that I needed to calm down, that I would be okay. I had been trained well, and Ms. Glickenhaus would not have asked me had she thought that I could not do it very well. "So calm down," she said, and plan what you are going to do. If you plan well, the lesson will go well. I had planned very well before, but I had never ever conducted a demonstration for veteran teachers. Ms. Glickenhaus came to visit me the day before the demonstration was scheduled to take place to help me plan, but I had already planned the lesson, made charts, and secured my pictures and other hands-on objects that I would need. She said that she did not need to help me because I had done a good job planning. She read the lesson plans, and the plans were easy for her to follow and were excellent. I was a little nervous, but I believed that if a teacher planned and organized well, the implementation would go well too. Ms. Glickenhaus praised my teaching style and told me that I would become an outstanding teacher. She said that lots of other teachers would be jealous of me because I was an excellent teacher. She told me that I sounded like a southern girl and that I needed to talk slower so that no one would notice my southern accent. The other teachers in the school told me that my demonstration lesson was outstanding, but later on in the year, they called me Ms. Glickenhaus's pet. I was the first teacher in the school who had been asked to conduct a demonstration lesson for the other teachers. The principal of the school also told me that I had done an outstanding job. She said that she knew that I was a good teacher when she saw me. She, too, believed that teachers were born and not made, and I was born to be a teacher. Of course, I did not believe such at the time, but today, I believe that teachers are born or called to the profession by God. In any case, I loved teaching, and I still do to this day. I do believe that teaching is both a science and an art. Teachers must know the content of the discipline and must develop their own teaching style to help others learn.

I remained at Nichols Avenue Elementary School from January 1965 until January 1967. My husband returned from a tour in Vietnam, and then we moved to Germany. When I found out that we were moving to Germany, I was so glad that while in college I had taken a course in German. At the time, I did not want to take the course, but when I registered for a foreign language, German was the only class that was available, so I ended up in the German class. I said at the time that I would never need such a course, so why spend my time and money in a German class. I never knew that I would end up in Germany. We moved to Germany in 1965, and remained there for one year. I taught first grade in the US Department of Defense schools in Germany. That was an interesting experience. There were no severe discipline problems, and the students were eager to learn.

While we were in Germany, we had our first baby girl. As soon as she was six months old, I started teaching her. I started pointing out her toes, hands, nose, mouth, ears, and eyes. Not too long after I started those lessons, she would point to each of the body parts as I called them out. She was learning as I was teaching. I continued to teach her as she grew and went to school. She was and has always been receptive to learning. Today, she is a lawyer and still learning.

We soon returned to the United States, and I went back to the District of Columbia school system. This time I was sent to Savory Elementary School to teach first grade. The students were eager to learn. This was a newly built school that had replaced the old Nicholas Avenue Elementary School. I met many new teachers there, and we have remained friends over the years. Ms. Barbara Snow, Ms. Bernice Sledge, and Ms. Marie White were also first grade teachers. Marie White and I went to Norfolk State College together, and we ended up teaching at the same school several times in our teaching careers. The principal of the school was a tall, slender lady named Ms. Betty Larkins. She and I got along very well. I had already learned from Ms. Alberta Beverly (deceased) what was expected of good teachers. In my first grade class, I taught mathematics twice each day. In fact, I taught geometry in the morning, and in the afternoon, I taught the District of Columbia's standards of mathematics. In fact, I integrated mathematics in everything that I taught. I liked the students, and they seemed to like me. They were all eager to learn. I made the class exciting, and I was excited about teaching, using hands-on activities and problem-solving strategies. I wrote very simple and easy-to-understand lesson plans that focused on the title of the lesson, the objectives, the motivating activities, the guided practice activities, the independent activities, and the assessment tasks. I summarized the lesson and focused on the assessment tasks that were used to show evidence that the students had learned the subjects taught,

I continued teaching in the District of Columbia school district until I went on maternity leave in 1970 for three years. When I was ready to return to work, I decided to try another school system. I applied for a teaching position in Prince George's County school district in Maryland because my family had recent moved there. I interviewed for the position and was offered a fourth grade class. I taught fourth grade for one year. I was in a high-earning socioeconomic neighborhood, and the students did very well. While I was teaching there, I decided to further my education. I enrolled in the graduate program at the University of Maryland in College Park. I never forgot how my teacher mentors at Norfolk State College had encouraged me to pursue a master's degree. I enrolled in the elementary education program with an emphasis in elementary school mathematics. I believe that at that time the University of Maryland was about the only or one of the few colleges/universities in the Washington and Maryland area that had an elementary school program with an emphasis in elementary school mathematics. This gave me another opportunity to pursue mathematics. The program required thirty-six graduate hours. I was working a full-time job and taking care of two children, so I enrolled as a part-time student, with six hours. The first course was a content course in algebra, and the second course was a course in the foundations of education. Six hours may not sound like a lot of work, but when you are working full-time and have two children and a husband to look after, it can be difficult to get everything done. Nevertheless, I was excited about the program.

At the end of the academic year, I returned to the District of Columbia school system as a first grade teacher. I did not finish the graduate program because my husband had been deployed on a second tour in Germany. This time when we were going to Germany, I requested a leave of absent from the school system so that when I returned, I would not be considered a new teacher. We moved to Germany and remained there for one year, and again I taught first grade in the US Department of Defense schools. This again was a very nice experience. The teaching and learning processes were the same. The biggest difference was the behavior of the students. These students were all children of military parents who were serving their country. Each military installation had its own school for the students of military families.

While I was in Germany, I continued to teach my own children. As most parents did, I read stories to them and taught them mathematics, using all kinds of hands-on activities, such as flash cards, spoons, or whatever objects I could find. I spent most of my time helping them understand geometry. You see, I think that if students understand geometric concepts and the world around them, they are more likely to have a better understanding of the other areas of mathematics. Research shows that geometry was the first mathematics that was actually recorded, if this is true, I do not understand why geometry appears near the end of most elementary school mathematics books. Teachers seem to have a difficult time teaching geometric concepts. This crisis may have been because elementary school teachers in general have a limited number of courses in mathematics. In fact, while working on this book, I discovered that a large number of teacher preparation programs require less than 12 hours of mathematics content for their prospective elementary school teachers.

CHAPTER 4
MASTER OF EDUCATION DEGREE

At the end of my husband's one-year tour, we returned to the United States. I took a teaching position in the District of Columbia school district. While working as an elementary school teacher, I decided to re-enroll in the master of education program at the University of Maryland. The first course I took covered the methods in teaching math-

ematics. It was called "Diagnostic and Remediation in Elementary School Mathematics," and it was taught by Dr. Robert Ashlock. He was an exciting professor of mathematics. He believed in using hands-on activities to teach mathematics. I did very well in the class. I received a "B," but I learned a lot about how to determine the strengths and weaknesses of students, which was something I did not know before this course. The course required a practicum, and we applied the theory by teaching and testing students. The school of education had established a mathematics laboratory for elementary school students. I worked in the laboratory two evenings a week for sixteen weeks with one student. The student had severe problems with understanding basic facts. In fact, to help the student, I posed simple problems for him to solve and used concrete objects to help him understand and remember the basic facts. The second course that I took was a science course for elementary school teachers. A female professor taught it, and she, too, was a hands-on professor. I took many other education courses, but the courses that I remember most are the courses in mathematics. I decided that I wanted a master's degree in education with an emphasis in elementary school mathematics, so the next course that I enrolled in was geometry. Then I took number theory, statistics, probability, and data analysis. I had already taken the content course in algebra, so I was right on track with the program. Ms. Geneva Knight, a former instructor at Hampton University, who was working on her doctorate in mathematics education, taught many of these courses. She was an excellent professor, and I learned a lot more about mathematics. I completed the master of education degree in May 1973, and I applied for a teaching position in the DC system as a mathematics resource teacher. I was selected as a mathematics resource teacher, and I was very excited. I thought that I was going to teach mathematics at the school to which I was assigned, but the principal needed a science teacher. Her thinking was that elementary school teachers can teach all subjects.

Science Resource Teacher

I was assigned to Drew Elementary School in Washington, DC. The principal of the school, whose name I do not remember thought I would be great in the position because I had an excellent background in mathematics. I then told her that I did not know much about science because I had taken a limited number of science courses while in college. She responded, "You can learn it." When I was in college, there was limited science equipment for elementary school teachers to use to conduct science experiments.

At that time I had not learned how to integrate mathematics with science, and I had not realized that mathematics could be used as a tool to teach science. Although I had been a classroom teacher, I had focused on the skills of reading, writing, and mathematics. I had not viewed mathematics from a problem-solving perspective. As I studied and taught more mathematics, I realized that a problem-solving approach was much more effective for student learning and retention.

I soon realized that I was going to teach science for the academic year. I decided that I had to learn the subject so that I could teach it. I found that the school had no science equipment or science kits available. I established a science lab and used what I could find to teach the students. I focused on the physical sciences first, and the students seemed to enjoy this area of science because they had an opportunity to learn something new, and it was hands-on using concrete objects, especially in measurement and the metric system. The fourth through sixth grade students came to the science lab on a regular basis. In fact, the sixth grade class was selected to participate in the science fair. I told the students that we had to represent Charles Drew Elementary School in the science fair. So the students and I put together a science project. I was not pleased with it, but I actually did not know what to do to make it better. We did not place at all in the assessment at the district level. One of the sixth grade teachers told me after the science fair was over that he thought that I could have done a better job. I held my breath to keep from saying something unkind, and then I told him that I could have used some help. In fact, I could have used his help since he was a science teacher. After that, he said nothing else to me about the science project. I struggled through the science program for the rest of the year. I think that the principal realized that science was not my specialty, so she asked me to serve as the mathematics resource teacher next semester. I was excited and served as the mathematics resource teacher at this school. The supervisor selected the best elementary school teachers throughout the school district, trained them in mathematics, and placed them in various schools. These resource teachers taught mathematics at the elementary school level and provided assistance to other teachers who needed help and additional resources.

Mathematics Resource Teacher

After I was selected to serve as a mathematics resource teacher, I was assigned to four schools. The first school was Aiton Elementary School. I was the only mathematics resource teacher selected who already held a master's degree. I was selected because I was an excellent teacher, and I also had credentials and training in mathematics. The director of mathematics believed that teachers had to be an excellent teacher first, and then they could be trained to teach mathematics more effectively. The director met with the resource teachers on Friday of each week to show them how to teach mathematics through the use of hands-on materials. I already knew everything that the director showed us, but I remained quiet and calm and never said a word. When I had an opportunity to demonstrate what I knew, I did very well. I remained a mathematics resource teacher in the District of Columbia from September 1974 until June 1987. Some of the mathematics resource teachers were assigned two schools, while others had up to five different schools. In my particular case, I was assigned to four elementary schools—Burville, Charles Drew, Charles Young, and Aiton. I taught mathematics to grades four, five, and six at each school. With the four schools, I taught mathematics one day a week, and on Fridays of each week, we met with the director of the elementary school mathematics program to continue more training in mathematics.

I was very happy when I went to Aiton Elementary School. The culture there was much more pleasant. In fact, one of the teachers I had met at Norfolk State College was teaching at Aiton. She was an excellent teacher, too. I served as the mathematics resource teacher and was very happy to be teaching mathematics.

I soon learned that mathematics was a tool for teaching science, but teaching science was never fun for me. I really think I disliked it because I did not know the curriculum and did not have the necessary science equipment and resources. As the mathematics resource teacher, my emphasis was on teaching mathematics in grades three through six. I thought that by the time the students were in third grade, they needed much more mathematics content. The program at Aiton Elementary School was a pull-out program wherein the students came to the mathematics lab three times a week to learn mathematics. This type of structure provided planning-time for the classroom teachers. I continued at Aiton Elementary School under Mr. Ronald Hasting, the principal of Aiton at the time. He left to take another principal position somewhere else in the district. Dr. Herman Roebuck was assigned as principal, and I remained as the mathematics resource teacher.

As a mathematics resource teacher, I organized the classes and motivated students so that they would like mathematics. The students appeared to be very excited about mathematics. I used hands-on activities, calculators, and many other manipulatives in my lessons. A typical day in my classroom included the following: The students would arrive at 9:15 a.m. and choose mathematics activities of their choice to work on for about twenty minutes. After about twenty minutes, I would (1) get the attention of all the students, (2) tell them what we were going to do, (3) show them how to do whatever the objectives were, (4) allow them to work in groups to achieve the objectives, (5) allow someone from each group to explain what was done, and (6) assign homework to review the skills that were taught. Many times when I selected a unit of study, I would read a story to the students about the topic, help them solve some problems relating to the topic, and allow the students to share what they did. For example, I usually started with a unit on geometry. I believed that students had to understand geometric concepts first, and then they could understand other branches of mathematics. I would read a story to the students about shapes in our world, talk to them about various shapes around us, show them different shapes, and provide time for them to name, describe, analyze, and solve word problems through the use of shapes. They would have to locate different kinds of shapes in our world. I started with the unit on shapes because I have always believed that if students understood geometric concepts, they could understand all other areas of mathematics. Most teachers never get a chance to actually teach geometry because they spend most of their time teaching whole numbers and fractions. Textbook companies seem to think that students only need to understand whole and rational number systems. I agree that students must understand the concept of numbers and learn how to apply the basic operations through the use of whole and rational numbers, but it seems to me that if students understand their own world through shapes, they can learn to count shapes, classify shapes, find patterns in shapes, combine geometric shapes, compare and contrast shapes, and measure shapes. Then they will have an easier time when they must understand the abstract concepts of geometry.

As a mathematics resource teacher, I conducted several workshops at Aiton Elementary School to show my peers how to teach problem-solving strategies, how to use calculators, and other hands-on activities to teach mathematics more effectively. In addition, while I was teaching at Aiton Elementary School, I wrote a proposal to teach problem-solving techniques through the use of calculators. This was an innovative idea in 1972. The proposal was funded, but many of my peers thought that if students used calculators, they would not learn the basic operations. To their surprise, these first grade students learned basic addition. As they repeatedly put the number combinations into the calculator, they were able to remember the basic facts and could determine if they put in the correct information to get the correct answer.

By September 1986, the District of Columbia had organized a program called "Building Resource Teachers." This program allowed master teachers to work with new teachers and those teachers whom the principal thought needed help. I remained as the mathematics resource teacher for one year. Then Dr. Herman Roebuck asked me to apply for the building resource teacher's position. The teacher who had been the previous building resource teacher and I got along very well, and then, when I was selected to be the new building resource teacher, she was not very happy. At first, I thought that it was going to be an exciting job, but I also had to continue to work with the students who needed help in mathematics. So actually, I wore two hats and had two positions, but only one paid. There was no increase in pay for the position either. I remained in the position for two years. Then the principal needed help, so I became the special assistant to the principal. Now I had three jobs. I helped him with the various activities and projects. Of course, some of the teachers began to dislike me, and some of them were not very nice.

I continued as the mathematics resource teacher, building resource teacher, and special assistant to the principal until the regional superintendent, Dr. Shelia Handy, heard about me, and she came to the school to observe me teaching. She asked me to serve as a peer resource teacher in order to help new and veteran teachers improve their teaching skills and techniques. I was excited, and I believed that I was an excellent teacher.

Peer Teacher Program

In between serving as a mathematics resource teacher, a building resource teacher, and a special assistant to the principal, the school district had implemented a peer teacher program. The supervisor from each region of the school district selected good teachers to show their peers how to be more effective in the classroom and how to best implement the newly designed curriculum. I served as a peer teacher from 1983 to 1984. The peer teacher program focused on selecting outstanding teachers to serve in the regional office to show other teachers how to implement the competency-based curriculum. The peer teachers conducted workshops for groups of teachers at the regional office or on site at their home schools. During the time of the peer program, many educators around the country were concerned about the metric system. I conducted numerous workshops with teachers, students, and parents using the metric system. At the risk of sounding immodest, I used the metric system in every workshop that I conducted, and my ratings from the workshop participants were outstanding. The presentations dealt with hands-on activities, and they were simple and understandable. The next year the peer teachers were sent to teach the seventh grade at the junior high school level. The administration believed that if elementary school teachers followed the sixth grade students to junior high school, they could help the students master the skills and concepts in mathematics. I served in this position for one year. I did not like the junior high students; therefore, I requested to return to the elementary school. I returned to Aiton Elementary School and resumed my teaching position as the mathematics resource teacher. I continued as the building resource teacher as well, and I ended up doing more administrative work because I was also working as the special assistant to the principal. I took on duties and activities that would have been assigned to an assistant principal had one been at the school. I continued to teach mathematics and to provide workshops for new teachers. Later in the academic year, teaching reading comprehension was added to my agenda. While reading was not my specialty, the principal thought that I could help new teachers become more successful in the classroom.

I wanted new teachers to know that the District of Columbia school system was and still is one of the state-of-the-art school districts in the United States. Even as I wrote this book, I observed some of the activities that were being implemented in the DC school system, and now when teachers talk to me about what innovative things they are doing in their classroom, I think about how I was doing many of those so-called innovations when I worked in the DC school system—writing student learning objectives, using hands-on activities, using cooperative learning groups, and writing detailed lesson plans. In fact, as I mentioned earlier, I wrote a proposal to teach problem-solving skills through the use of calculators. Despite pushback and skepticism, the students learned how to solve problems and what they needed to input into the calculator to get the correct answer. The calculator was just a tool to enhance learning, the same way the pencil was a tool long time ago. Again, I was a visionary teacher, and the principal almost fired me when he found out I was using calculators. He did not understand the effectiveness of these lessons until he observed me in the class. Then he was able to understand the teaching process when he saw how well the first grade students were doing. In fact, he was more pleased when the students took the California or the Iowa Test of Basic Skills because my first grade students ended up outperforming the other first graders in mathematics and reading in the school.

Although I liked teaching and was comfortable as a teacher, I had a long-term goal of becoming more educated, and I wanted a doctorate degree. I actually had a deep desire to become a college professor. In fact, I thought that I would be more effective in training students to become teachers. As I continued to serve as the building resource teacher and mathematics resource teacher, I decided to return to school to pursue a doctorate degree.

I had always wanted a doctorate, but I was not sure about the best way to pay for it. So I started to look for scholarships and fellowships. I landed a full fellowship at American University (AU) in Washington, DC. The college of education at AU had a grant program designed to increase the minority population at the doctoral level. I wrote an essay explaining the reasons I wanted a doctorate degree, and then I interviewed for the fellowship. I soon received a full fellowship to complete the doctorate of philosophy degree in educational administration.

CHAPTER 5
DOCTORATE OF PHILOSOPHY DEGREE

I started graduate school to work on my doctorate degree at the American University in Washington, DC, in September, 1984. I studied educational administration with support fields in gifted education, curriculum, instruction and assessment, and training and development. As my goal, I wanted to teach at the university level so that I could influence the training and development of young teachers, particularly in the way teachers taught mathematics at the elementary and middle school levels.

American University was an exciting place for me. There were students from all over the world in my graduate level classes. They were teachers, principals, supervisors, or other administrators from various ethnic groups. Everyone was very serious about completing the degree in order to move to the next level in his or her career. My first class was a course on the foundations of administration. This was an interesting class because it focused on the school as a social institution as well as the philosophical, psychological, and social issues that often affected public schools. The professor who taught the course was an administrator in the District of Columbia government. He lectured, but he also provided opportunities for the students to ask questions. I enjoyed the class and learned a lot about administration and leadership. I had always been on a quest for knowledge. In fact, I had been taking courses since I had completed my bachelor's degree. I arrived on the campus of American University with about eighty graduate hours in courses that ranged from mathematics, curriculum, instruction, assessment, and gifted education, to leadership from various colleges and universities, including the District of Columbia Teachers College, Trinity College, Bowie State College, and Howard University. The other classes at the American University included curriculum development, instructional strategies, budget analysis, program evaluation, training and development, administrative effectiveness, and statistics. I was required to complete a total of forty-two hours beyond the master's degree, considering that I had come to American University with eighty hours beyond a bachelor's degree. My areas of concentration for the doctorate included curriculum, instruction, and assessment, and gifted education. I was not required to take additional courses if I could pass the comprehensive examination in curriculum and in gifted education. The examination in curriculum consisted of a written test, and the examination in gifted education was an oral test. One of the main questions that my committee asked me was how I would go about developing curriculum, instruction, and assessment for young students who had been incarcerated. While the question seemed unusual at first, I thought about it for a few seconds. Then I realized that in my opinion, some of the crimes that some young people commit are planned by master minds, and if these same students had opportunities to focus on other challenging activities, they may not have committed such crimes. In fact, one of my daughters could have had severe behavior problems in the regular public schools if I had not been on top of the situation. I had her tested, and her IQ was almost off the chart. The work that her teachers had been trained to give students was not challenging enough for her, and she would finish in a hurry and start talking. I ended up putting her in a private school where the teacher would challenge her and where she could not speed through her work. Now she had to think and write rather than just fill in blanks on paper. Today, she is doing well because she was challenged to think critically and solve problems. In fact, she is a teacher and has been promoted to a science curriculum specialist for the Next Generation Science Program in the school district where she works,

My program of study at American University focused on the administration of gifted education. Every course that I took focused on gifted education, and every paper that I presented emphasized gifted education in some way. For example, when I completed a project that dealt with the budget, it always dealt with a budget for a gifted education program. I followed the same pattern with my project on curriculum and program evaluation. My dissertation focused on problems and solutions in administrating a gifted education program. I completed all the requirements for the doctorate degree and defended my dissertation in December 1987. I was very happy that now I could train teachers. Training teachers for me meant being able to teach at the college level or at the higher education academy.

Now back to my work. I remained at Aiton Elementary School until June 1987. I had always wanted to teach at the university level because I wanted to train and develop future teachers. After I completed the doctorate degree, I decided that I wanted to train teachers. I had always considered myself a visionary and transformational leader. Rather than apply to the search committee to find a position, I wrote directly to the president of the college, Dr. William R. Harvey. He responded and told me that he was sending my application to the dean of the school of education. At that time, one of my daughters was a student at this university, so

I went down to the university for parents' weekend. While I was on the campus, I had an opportunity to meet Dr. Carlton Brown. God opened the door for me to meet him. I was at the luncheon, and when Dr. Brown arrived, the only vacant seat in the room was next to me, which I had saved for my purse. We talked, and then I asked him if there were any vacancies on the campus. He proceeded to tell me that he was already going to interview a candidate next week. He said if that interview was not successful, he would look at other candidates. We ate and continued to talk about the campus. Before I left, I gave him one of my cards with my name and contact information. He looked at it, and I began to smile. I had no idea at the time that I was being considered for an interview. After we laughed for a bit, he asked me when could I interview, and I said Monday. I called the principal of my school in DC and informed him that I needed to take personal leave on Monday. I interviewed, and about two weeks later, I received a letter and a contract for employment at Hampton University. Well, I accepted the position as an assistant professor in the school of education. During my career at Hampton University, I learned much as a person and as an administrator. I had the wonderful opportunity to work with people like William R. Harvey, who was and still is the president of Hampton University; Dr. Martha Dawson (now deceased), who was the vice president of academic affairs; and Dr. Mary Christian, who was dean of education for a short time when I arrived on the campus.

CHAPTER 6
TEACHING AT THE
UNIVERSITY LEVEL

I accepted the position as a faculty member in the school of education. I arrived at Hampton University on July 1, 1987. I was afraid of college students. I felt apprehensive because undergraduate students still thought that they knew everything, and many of them believed that you, the instructor, are there to teach only them. They do not know that professors have other opportunities and obligations other than teaching, and I quickly learned this lesson.

My first four classes at Hampton University covered foundations of education, human growth and development, teaching in the secondary schools, and teaching mathematics at the secondary level. While I was excited about the education courses, I was more  excited about the courses covering the methods of teaching mathematics. I immediately had a flashback to my days in a mathematics classroom at the elementary and middle school levels. I remembered that the students in my class had a difficult time understanding mathematics, and the teacher never used any concrete objects to help the students understand the concepts. Sure, many high school teachers believed in Piaget's theory—that is, by the time that students are at the high school level, they should be able to think abstractly. That may be true, but some students do not have good spatial skills and have not matured enough to think abstractly. They probably have not studied enough mathematics that relates to real-life situations; therefore, they often fail these classes. Should students fail mathematics because they have difficulty thinking abstractly when they have not had enough experience in learning the concepts? My answer is unequivocally no. Students should be taught using hands-on activities at the level they feel comfortable if they do not understand the concepts. They may not understand now because their elementary and middle school teachers may not have understood the mathematics well enough to teach it so that the students understood the subjects and could master the standards.

Teaching mathematics at the secondary school level was an exciting course for me. The students in the class were mathematics majors who would teach at the high school level. They had come through their college years thinking that one had to be smart to teach mathematics. Well, when they met me in the class, I told them that even if they were teaching calculus, they would need to make the mathematics applicable to real-life situations for the students to understand and retain the information. I taught them to include problem-solving skills and relate the problems to the real lives of the students. The students in my class did not want to do that kind of work. They just wanted to teach mathematics at the high school level in the same manner in which they were taught in high school or college. Well, I operated on the premise that America was facing a crisis in mathematics education, and research showed that the achievement scores in geometry, problem solving, and estimation were lower for students in the United States than they were for students in other industrialized countries of the world (US Department of Education, 1988). They were not interested in my statistics or research. They just wanted to breeze through the course, but I made sure they did not. Every lesson that they taught, they had to use a problem-solving base and show how it related to the real lives of the students. I showed them how to develop lesson plans based on the "tell, show, and do" strategy and how to use concrete objects to get the concepts across to students. I also showed them how to design units, how to construct teaching charts and boards, and how to manage a mathematics classroom with different cooperative learning groups. I had high expectations that if these students would begin to change the way mathematics was taught in their own classrooms, then the achievement level of students would improve. I really had no way of knowing, but what I did know was that mathematics education in the United States needed to improve. Teachers needed to be trained on how to use concrete objects and abstract activities to help students learn mathematics.

I entered Hampton University in July 1987 as an assistant professor, and I remained at the university until June 30, 1998. While I was working at Hampton University, I wrote several proposals and published several articles, all of which eventually culminated in me receiving tenure. I received $300,000 from the National Aeronautical and Science Administration (NASA) to improve the mathematics and science skills of pre-college students. I received $200,000 from the Virginia Department of Education and $100,000 from the Virginia Common Wealth of High Education to train and mentor cooperating teachers and to supervise student teachers. During my first summer at Hampton University, I worked in the NASA Education Center and wrote curriculum that teachers could use to help students understand what NASA did and how important the space program was to the world. In July 1991, I was also asked to serve as the instructional leader of the Hampton University's laboratory school. As director of the Hampton University's laboratory school, I continued to dabble in teaching. I taught a class each semester and during the summer. I also taught mathematics for one hour per week to students in grades three through five in the laboratory school. I became the instructional leader for the laboratory school on July 1, 1991. It has been my privilege and high honor to serve as the director of the Hampton University's laboratory school. When Ms. Julia Williams retired and turned over the keys to the laboratory school, symbolically transferring the powers and the burdens of the position on August 28, 1991, I had no idea how awesome the responsibility would be. Just trying to motivate the teachers to effect change and to manage the daily activities and budget of the school as an instructional leader was a full-time job. When I arrived, I had a vision of what I wanted to see in the laboratory school. I wanted to build upon the foundation Mrs. Julia Williams, Dr. Martha Dawson, Dr. Mary Christian, and others some 125 years earlier had laid. I wanted to involve the teachers in the decision-making process so that we would be prepared to lead the laboratory school into the twenty-first century. I wanted the school to develop its own standards of learning that exceeded those developed by the Virginia Department of Education.

In large measure, I met most of these goals before I left, but admittedly, there was more work to finish. Teachers needed more training. They wanted higher salaries, more science and mathematics materials, and more teaching assistants in the classroom. The problem was that the school could not sustain itself based on the tuition the parents paid. However, the laboratory school became a leader in the use of the whole-language approach to teaching and learning, teaching mathematics, and using a problem-solving approach to mathematics and science. Teachers attended workshops on using the whole-language approach to teaching in the classroom. Of course, much of the finished work is not the product of one person in the laboratory school. All the teachers played a significant role in our accomplishments. I often think of the support that I received from Dr. Carlton Brown (the dean of the school of education at that time), Mrs. Julia Williams (former director), Dr. Martha Dawson (former vice president for academic affairs), Dr. Mary Christian (former dean of the school of education), and the teachers in the laboratory school. Their help was invaluable. I will always be indebted to my dedicated and loyal staff in the school as well. But most of all, I was indebted to the many volunteers who worked in the school and made the Extended Day Program a reality. I will always be very grateful for all of their assistance. To the president of Hampton University, Dr. William R. Harvey, and to my colleagues who believed in my leadership, I simply say that I have been honored by your confidence in me and for your help in making a difference at Hampton University's laboratory school. I have always tried to do what was right. I remember the encouraging words of Dr. Carlton Brown, former president of Savannah State University and former president of Clark Atlanta University. He would say, "Don't worry about criticism, for only one who has done nothing and accomplished nothing in life is free from the darts and arrows of criticism. So always strive to do your best."

Ultimately, we can view the progress in Hampton University's laboratory school as a change in the education of students within the twenty-first century. The mission was to change the way future teachers were educated, developed, and trained. My leadership approach continued to motivate teachers and students so that they believed in themselves and met the challenges of change in the twenty-first century.

In addition to being the instruction leader/director of Hampton University's laboratory school, I was an assistant professor in the school of education. As an assistant professor, I taught classes in the school of education, wrote several proposals that brought in more than $500,000, presented at conferences and conventions, and conducted workshops for other faculty members on teacher preparation.

The administration did not want to raise the tuition, so the laboratory school was closed. Some people blamed me, but I understood. There just were not enough funds to sustain its operation. When it closed, I went back to the school of education as a full-time faculty member. Although an assistant professor normally would be eligible to apply for tenue in the fifth year at the college, I decided to apply for tenue after four years. However, I was told by the administration that it was too early, so I applied again in my fifth year. Then I received tenure and was promoted to associate professor. I continued teaching courses in the school of education. When Dr. Carlton Brown left the deanship and became vice president for planning at Hampton University, another dean was selected. Her name was Dr. Helen Stiff. She was an excellent dean. She had lots of administrative experience in the Virginia State Department of Education prior to serving as the dean of education. When I met her, it did not take her very long to ascertain what kind of teacher I was. I remained at Hampton University until June 30, 1999.

CHAPTER 7
DEAN OF EDUCATION

I served as an associate professor of education at Hampton University for over five years, then, I got the idea that I wanted to be a dean because I thought that I could do what I saw Dr. Carlton Brown doing at the time. I applied for a position as director of teacher education and associate dean at North Carolina Central University. I interviewed for the position and started on July 1, 1999. When I became the assistant dean of education, I had just left one liberal arts college where I had been an associate professor of education for fourteen years, and now I was entering unknown territory in another liberal arts college. While I did not consult with other deans before I took the position, I had watched very closely what Dr. Carlton Brown had done at Hampton University as the dean of education. I had also observed Dr. Mary T. Christian and Dr. Helen Stiff, who became the dean of the school of education after Dr. Carlton Brown was appointed to a vice-president's position

at Hampton University. They seemed to have a great time, so I decided that I wanted to be a dean. I embarked upon a search. I landed an assistant dean's position at a historically black liberal arts college (HBCU) in Durham, North Carolina. As an assistant dean and director of student teaching, I thought I needed to know which decisions I had to make quickly, which ones I did not need to act on right away, and which ones could stand to wait. Because I had read about what it meant to be a dean, I thought that I was ready. I figured that I would not move too quickly. Instead I would take some time to get to know the dean and the faculty. I observed personalities and wanted to listen to the faculty and staff. I valued talking with faculty and students, but the dean of education thought that I was not doing anything but talking. The dean of education was busy talking about research, special conferences, and student-faculty research projects. I did not know if she listened to faculty members about their needs and concerns, but I could tell that she was not listening to me, so after one year I decided to leave. Obviously we had philosophical differences in what we thought an assistant dean should be doing and what she wanted me to do. She never told me what she expected, so I concentrated on finding placements for the student teachers and writing grants. I was trying to learn the culture of the university. The university had a president who was a lawyer, and I thought that I knew how lawyers operated. After all, I had three lawyers in the family who were visionaries and transformational leaders. I thought that I needed to learn what the faculty, staff, and students valued in the university. I read the mission statement, vision, goals, and strategic plans, and I used those to make all of my decisions. But I still had not learned the culture. I could not understand the ephemeral tone and tenor of the office of the dean, although I listened, watched, and tried to remember everything that was going on. Several faculty members came to me and said, "Why do you dress up to come to work?" I was surprised by the question. I had just completed leadership training and had learned that one should always look professional. I thought a suit, dress, or pant suits with a blouse looked professional, but I often encountered unprofessional behavior from the dean. She began to complain about everything that I did, so I knew that it was time to leave. If you are being harassed on a job, that's how you know that it is time for you to transfer to another school or seek a higher positon.

I served as the assistant dean of the school of education and director of teacher education for one year. In this position, my primary job was to make sure that the student teachers met the state educational requirements so that they could go into the field to do student teaching. I placed the student teachers—about ten that year—in various schools throughout the Durham area. I also assigned faculty members as university mentors to the student teachers. In addition, I visited each one about three times in the semester to make sure the student teachers were on task and were doing what was expected of them in the classroom.

The boss and I (the employee) were not on the same wavelength, so I made the first move to find another job. After all, I had read the book *What They Don't Tell You at the Harvard Business School.* I saw the signs and sense a difference in our philosophies. I just did not fit the culture under her leadership, so I sought another position. I found a position for an associate dean for the school of professional programs at Benedict College in Columbia, South Carolina. Perhaps it was unconventional, but I wrote a letter to the president of Benedict College and asked him if an associate dean had already been selected. If not, I told him, I would like the opportunity to interview for the position. He sent my application to the search committee, and I was soon called in for an interview. I interviewed for the position along with four other people on the same day. When we were all returning to the airport in the same vehicle, the three men tried to have a conversation about the position. I did not say anything, except I did tell the men that it was nice to meet them. About two weeks later, Dr. John Cole, acting dean of the school of professional programs, called and asked me if I would be interested in the associate dean's position. I said yes to the position. When I left North Carolina Central University, I was the assistant dean of the school of education. In higher education, an associate dean/professor is a higher rank than assistant, so I had been promoted. I arrived on campus of Benedict College on July 1, 2000. Benedict College was a very nice place to serve. I worked under Dr. John Cole as the associate dean of the school of professional programs. He told me that associate deans just helped the dean. So I waited for him to tell me what he wanted me to do. While I was waiting to find out what he wanted, I talked to people and got to know other faculty members on the campus. While I was facilitating this process, I met the vice president for academic affairs, Dr. Juanita Simon Scott. She was a very nice lady, but she was also strict and to the point. For some reason, she took a liking to me, and she assigned me to various committees—the Academic Affairs Committee, the Council of Deans Committee, the Honors and Founder's Day Committee, the Southern Association of Colleges and Schools Committee (SACS), and the Commencement Committee. She also assigned me to design an advising handbook for incoming freshman. I did all these duties, but it seemed that Dr. John Cole did not want me to serve on these committees. He never told me what projects he wanted me to work on. All I knew was that he never talked to me or met with me. I thought the dean and associate dean should—and would—meet to plan and strategize about how to move the school of professional programs into the twenty-first century. I continued to make friends with the faculty in the school of professional programs. At that time, Benedict did not have a school of education. It had a department of education, and Dr. Betty Caldwell Stukes was the chairperson. She and I got along very well as colleagues.

Benedict College was going through its evaluation and accreditation, and on many nights, Dr. Scott required the committee members to work at the college all night. After the evaluation and accreditation process, the president of the college assigned me to teach two classes. The department needed more faculty members. However, the dean of the school of professional programs did not want me to teach. He wanted me to serve as assistant dean after I informed him that I needed to set up office hours before and after class. Because the office of the associate dean was so small, I informed him that I needed to establish an office in the department of education. This meant that I would not be in the dean's office for two days out of the week. Instead I would be working with students on those days. The vice president for academic affairs said that I needed to spend more time helping the students, so I did. I remained at Benedict College until June 30, 2002.

My daughter was on the airplane to Philadelphia when she met the president of Cheyney University. She told him that her mother (me) wanted to be a dean. He told her that the university was searching for a dean of education and that I could send my credentials. I submitted my credentials to him, and in turn, he passed my resume onto the search committee. Soon I interviewed for the position, and shortly thereafter, I was employed as the dean of education at Cheyney University on July 1, 2002.

I did not learn how to lead at the right moment until I actually became the dean of education at Cheyney University of Pennsylvania. I had learned by then that the *dean* had a responsibility to motivate the faculty so that they want to make the school of education a better place. I also knew that I had to take the blame for problems that occurred.

In my research, I found that many deans had actually written about becoming deans, and many of them said that any person thinking about becoming a dean should ask him or herself, "Why do I want to become a dean?" They said that professors should ask themselves what the rewards and challenges of a deanship are and when is the right time to become a dean. A dean is an intellectual leader, administrator, fund-raiser, mentor, diplomat, problem solver, and member of the faculty. Faculty members who have never been deans do not realize the number of problems and challenges deans encounter (Johnson, 2009). The dean's position is a political one.

By the time I became the dean of education at Cheyney University, I had learned that I needed a sense of humor on top of my traditional responsibilities. Faculty members and students would have good and bad days, and as dean, I needed to be able to laugh when things were good and not so good. As the dean, I attended many long meetings as early as 7:30 a.m., as the president required his cabinet and deans to attend these meetings during early registration times. I also learned that progress was very slow in higher education. Faculty and staff did not want to change, which also made progress difficult. No wonder the secretary of education, Arne Duncan (July, 2014), said that schools of education were just cash cows, designed to get money, but not meeting the demands of a changing society. In fact, he also said that they should simply close down. I wrote an article that was published in the *Journal of the National Association of University Women* that focused on how deans of education should restructure and rethink teacher preparation programs.

When I arrived at Cheyney University, the school of education was in the process of losing its accreditation with the National Council of Accreditation of Teacher Educators (NCATE). I moved very quickly to establish a plan that would give the school more time to improve and to get students to pass Praxis I. The Praxis I test was one of the problems, not only at Cheyney University, but across the United States. The council accepted my plan, and in September 2002, the faculty and I put the plan in place. The plan was to restructure a course for education majors to focus on reading, writing, and mathematics. The Praxis I test consisted of these very subjects. When I arrived at Cheyney University, only 17 percent of the students in the teacher preparation program at the junior level had passed Praxis I, although there were about three hundred students in the program. The majority of the students who wanted to be teachers had difficulty passing the required tests to enter into the teacher preparation program. The students were very weak in reading, writing, and mathematics. After one year, the pass rate of the students in the teacher preparation program rose from 17 percent to 100 percent. I personally worked with the students to strengthen their test-taking skills and to help them learn the subject areas. While I was working at Cheyney University, I wrote several proposals, and they were funded in the amount of 2.5 million dollars. The funds came from the United States Department of Human Services, the Pennsylvania Department of Education, and the Tom Joyner Foundation in order to improve the Praxis I and Praxis II pass rate of education majors, and establish the Call Me Mister Program at Cheyney University. Soon a young African-American male was hired to serve as the director of the Call Me Mister Program. He had previously graduated from the Call Me Mister Program at Clemson University in South Carolina, where the original program had begun. I remained at Cheyney University for six years.

After President Clinton Pettus retired, Wallace Arnold, a retired military general became president of Cheyney University. He served as the president for four years. After he retired, a female took over the presidency. When she first arrived on the campus, she met with all of the faculty members and the previous deans one-on-one. When she met with me as dean of education, I told her that I was very pleased that she had come to Cheyney University, and I would help her in any way that I could. I had just remarried, but I would stay on for a few more years until the Call Me Mister Program was up and running smoothly. I decided to leave in January 2010. I moved to Columbia, South Carolina to be with my family and to take the deanship at Claflin University.

We worked hard to make changes at Cheyney University and to keep the school of education from losing its teacher education accreditation. After that, I realized that my six years as dean had been very exciting and rewarding, but very frustrating, too. When I became the dean of education, I had hoped that the lives I touched, the ideas that I shared, and the energy that I invested with others would make Cheyney University a better place. I know that deans come and go, and now I know why. When I became the Dean at Claflin University in Orangeburg, South Carolina, I came in trying to understand personalities of the faculty, trying to learn the culture of the school of education, and trying to lead at the right moment, all while maintaining a sense of humor. I remained as dean of education at Claflin University for eighteen months, and I decided to retire after that because my husband had recently retired. We decided to travel, and we have now traveled to every continent except Australia and Antarctica. However, we have plans to visit Australia very soon.

While I was working at Cheyney University and Claflin University, I was always asking the faculty what were the most effective strategies for training and preparing preservice teachers. I would also ask, "To what extent does knowledge of the subject matter contribute to the effectiveness of preservice teachers? Is there a significant advantage to having a preservice teacher preparation program as opposed to just having a graduate-level preparation program for preservice teachers? To what extent does pedagogical knowledge and skills improve preservice teacher's effectiveness?" These were some questions that I constantly answered as dean of education. I did not get much support until I left Cheyney and Claflin, and so I decided to conduct some research on my own. However, I did not publish my results until I retired from Claflin University.

I arrived on the campus of Claflin University on January 3, 2010, to take over the school of education. My first task was to meet with all of the faculty members and to find out what the major challenges were. The faculty members were rather new and very young. As I listened to the faculty, I realized they needed guidance. The pass rate in four years had been only 10 percent of the students enrolled in the teacher preparation program. Actually, only ten students had passed Praxis I in four years, yet there were about three hundred students in the program. Claflin's teacher preparation program seemed no different than other schools around the country, but only a few students had met the state requirements to enter the teacher preparation program. So after we assessed the situation, we determined that we needed to offer a course on Praxis I reading, writing, and mathematics. One of the professors taught the class, and I worked with the students in mathematics.

At the end of December 2010, thirty students had passed Praxis I. I was indeed happy because that meant that we could induct thirty students into the teacher preparation program. In addition to serving as the dean of education, I taught one course in the graduate program. I always wanted to keep my hands in teaching. Claflin University was a very exciting place to serve. The president, Dr. Henry Tisdale, was a visionary leader like me. I drove from Blythewood to Orangeburg every day, and after eighteen months I decided to retire. I retired from Claflin University in July 2011, and I decided to become an adjunct professor in the school of education at Southern Wesleyan University. After I retired, I decided to re-activate the G and H Educational and Research Foundation, Inc., a consulting firm. That way I could do some writing and consulting with school districts and other colleges about Praxis I. After all, I had been very successful in helping students pass Praxis I.

I began to write about teacher preparation. I thought that future teachers needed to study more mathematics, science, and reading, so I published the article "A New Direction for Teacher Education: A Paradigm Shift" in the spring 2013 in the *Journal of the National Association of University Women*. After the article was published, I received several invitations to make presentations about my research at conferences and conventions. I presented my research at the 2012 and 2013 Convention of the American Middle School Association. I continued to look for conferences to present my research and write articles about teacher preparation. After I retired for three years, I needed to do something exciting. I still wanted to be a teacher. I established the National Minority Girls Academy for young girls in grades four through six. This organization was designed to improve the academic and social skills of young girls. The girls met one Saturday a month for a year. During the summers, they were involved in a six-week academic academy that focused on reading, writing, mathematics, and social skills. The monthly program continued until I took an administrative position at Morris College during spring, 2015.

CHAPTER 8

GREAT TEACHERS, WHO MOTIVATED, INSPIRED, ENCOURAGED, AND COACHED ME

In my years of wanting to be a teacher, I have had personal encounters with brilliant educators who motivated, inspired, coached, and/or mentored me so that I could become a great teacher. I have included some of these educators in my book to let others know that I stood on the shoulders of giants, and I want others to stand on my shoulders so that they can be successful too.

Ms. R. L. Stamps

Ms. R. L. Stamps (deceased) was a great friend who was concerned about me. She was an excellent educator in her own rights from Emporia, Virginia. She was a teacher, educator, and supervisor. She taught, inspired, and motivated students to pursue college degrees, even some in teaching. She was an educator until she passed away at the age of ninety-seven. She was very much concerned about me and what I was going to do with my life. She inspired me to go to college, even when my family had no money and was not formerly educated. She continued to say, "You are smart, so you need to go to college, and you will make a great teacher". So, I went to college to become a teacher.

Ms. Leslie Smith Cobb

Ms. Leslie Smith Cobb was and still is my mentor, friend, and mother. She was an excellent teacher from Norfolk, Virginia, where she taught for thirty years. She inspired and motivated students to love learning. She was such a great elementary school teacher who became a district lead teacher in Norfolk, a district-level supervisor, and a personnel director. She focused on hiring the best teachers for Norfolk Public Schools. She, too, has been a prominent educator, teacher, and consultant. At the age of ninety-six, she continues to educate, train, and develop anyone who listens to her. She inspired, motivated, coached, mentored, and encouraged me to be an excellent teacher. I became a great teacher.

Ms. Lucinda Smith

Ms. Lucinda Smith was my cooperating teacher when I engaged in student teaching as a senior at Norfolk State University. She was a first grade teacher in the Norfolk public school system. She was a prominent teacher, and her principal selected her to train student teachers. She was an excellent teacher and leader who had the knowledge, skills, and disposition to ensure that her students learned. She was a very quiet and soft-spoken teacher who commanded respect from her students and everyone around her. I learned much from her on how to plan, implement, and assess what students learned. Her philosophy said that unless students learned, no teaching had actually taken place. I, too, believe that statement still holds true today.

Dr. Mary Christian

Dr. Mary Christian was the dean of education when I went to Hampton University in 1988 to serve on the faculty in the school of education. I got to know her and admired her very much. She had outstanding qualities that made her an excellent teacher. She was an elementary school teacher in Hampton, Virginia in her earlier years. She received her bachelor's degree from Hampton University, and she went on to earn a doctorate in education. She taught in the public schools and later decided that she wanted to train teachers. She served Hampton University for thirty years until she retired. In 1988, when I went to Hampton University, Dr. Christian taught me that life's battles do not always go to the smartest, the prettiest, or the strongest. The person who wins the battle is the one who believes that she can win. She also said that a woman must believe in herself before others can believe in her. Dr. Christian became my role model, and she also taught me that one must be prepared to offer a vision and solutions. She said that the vision must be one of empowerment, taking those who have lost their sense of family and empowering them with a sense of pride and responsibility. She became a prominent educator, leader, administrator, professor, and delegate. She celebrated her ninetieth birthday in July 2014 on the campus of Hampton University.

Ms. Martha Elizabeth Cunningham Monteith

I met this outstanding teacher when I moved to South Carolina. She was a member of the National Association of University

Women (NAUW), and I became very impressed with her as I talked with her about teaching. She, too, was a prominent teacher in the Richland One School District in Columbia, South Carolina, where she had worked for more than thirty years. She received a Bachelor of Arts degree in speech from Allen University. She later received a master's degree in speech pathology, and she did further study at various colleges and universities around the country. I admired her when I met her, and after I talked with her over a period of time, I realized that she was a renowned educator in the Richland School District One. The Richland School District One inducted her into the Richland One Hall of Fame because she had been such an outstanding teacher in the district.

Ms. Naomi Joann Hall Dresher

I met Ms. Dresher while I was working at Benedict College in Columbia, South Carolina, and I became very impressed with her. Every time I talked with her, she was always very inspiring. She motivated me to continue to be an outstanding educator. As I talked with her, I realized that she had the qualities that made her an outstanding teacher, and I wanted to be like her. She, too, taught for more than thirty years in the Richland One School District. After she retired from the district, she decided to make her mark on student teachers. She joined the school of education at Benedict College, where she served for more than ten years in training, inspiring, and motivating students to pursue teacher education and become great teachers. She received a Bachelor of Arts degree in English from Benedict College. After she graduated from Benedict College, she realized that she was called to teach, so she attended South Carolina State University to obtain a master's degree in elementary education. She, too, believed that she needed to remain current in the field of education, so she attended several other universities across the United States. She was such a great teacher that the superintendent of Richland One School District tapped her to become a social studies consultant and an elementary education consultant to provide guidance to new teachers in the school district.

After she retired from Richland School District One, she became a professor at Benedict College, where she established a program to increase the number of males pursuing degrees in elementary education. The program was called Minority Access to Teacher Education (MATE). She is a prominent educator who believes that she is supposed to help others as she passes through this world. At the age of ninety, she is still smiling, teaching, inspiring, and motivating students to pursue careers in education.

Dr. Louvenia Magee

Dr. Louvenia Magee, too, was a prominent teacher, first in the District of Columbia public school system and then in Prince George's County, Maryland. She was a science teacher, and she loved teaching. She knew that students did not know much science in general, and many of them were not interested in science anyway. Her job was to make science exciting so that students would learn. She was such a great teacher that she was voted teacher of the year in the District of Columbia Public Schools. She continued teaching in the system until she retired. After she retired, she realized she loved teaching so much that she went to work as an elementary school teacher in Prince George's County Public Schools, where she currently teaches. She makes sure that her students are able to read, understand mathematics, science, and social studies, and enjoy school.

I have been impressed with her work as a teacher for a very long time. We knew each other as children in the Virginia and North Carolina area. We met again in the District of Columbia school system where we taught for over 15 years. She was a science teacher, and I was a mathematics teacher. She inspired me to go to graduate school to obtain a doctorate degree in education. She had already received her doctorate in education and was pursuing her dream of becoming an outstanding educator.

Ms. Marie White Barfield

Ms. Marie White Barfield was a prominent sixth grade teacher in the District of Columbia. She attended Norfolk State College in Norfolk, Virginia, where she studied elementary education. She was an excellent student and had the knowledge, skills, and disposition to be an effective teacher. We were classmates at Norfolk State University, and we were initiated into the same sorority at the same time. I admired her because she was always so well organized and efficient. We ended up in the same school in the District of Columbia school system. She was a sixth grade teacher, and I was a first grade teacher. She had a very strong command and presence, which allowed her to better deal with sixth grade students. She retired from the District of Columbia school system after thirty years of service to her students and her community. She was outstanding because she possessed the characteristics of an effective teacher.

Dr. Gertrude Henry, Professor
Emeritus at Hampton University

I met Dr. Henry when I interviewed for the position at Hampton University in 1988. She asked me a bold question, "Why do you want to teach at Hampton University?" I responded by saying that I thought that I was an outstanding public school teacher. Plus I did not like what I saw in the teachers in the District of Columbia school system, so I wanted to train teachers to help them become better teachers. I also said that I had been viewed as an outstanding teacher myself, so I wanted to impart some of my knowledge and skills about teaching to prospective teachers. In addition, many people viewed Hampton University as an outstanding college to train teachers, and I wanted to be a part of the cutting edge at the university. Well, the dean hired me, and I was most pleased. When I arrived on the campus, Dr. Henry befriended me, and we have been professional and personal friends for more than twenty-five years. I observed her on several occasions in the classroom while I was at Hampton, and she was an outstanding educator. She knew how to motivate college students, and she was very strict about what she thought that new teachers should know. She taught me that I needed to be concerned about the success of my students and always make sure that they understood how they could be successful in the classroom. So too, her presentations were well planned, very exciting, and well executed. Her assessments were always in line with the objectives that she taught.

Ms. Glenda Cathine Gilchrist-Pinkett

Glenda is my daughter, and she also chose to become a teacher. I view her as an outstanding teacher. I think that she became a teacher because I was a teacher. She went to the same school where I taught in the District of Columbia, and one of my Norfolk State colleagues, Ms. Marie White Barfield, was her teacher. Glenda was very impressed with Ms. Marie White Barfield, although she talked a lot in the class. But the teacher was able to motivate and inspire her. I also mentored, coached, inspired, and motivated her to always do an excellent job in the classroom. It has paid off. As of now, she is the Secondary Science Curriculum Coordinator for the Christiana Public School District. I included her because I still view her as a young teacher, although she has been teaching for about sixteen years. She received a Bachelor of Science degree in biology from Hampton University. She is currently working on a master's degree in curriculum, instruction, and assessment, and she has aspirations of becoming an expert curriculum specialist.

When she first started as a young teacher, I spent a week with her in the classroom to make sure that she got off to a great start. She planned very well. Her plans were well written in very simple details to make sure that the person who read them would understand what needed to be done. Most high school teachers had been trained to believe that the arrangement of seats did not matter, but when I observed her students, I immediately told her to put all of the noisemakers and those students who appeared to want attention in the front of the room near her desk. She tried it, and it worked. Over the years, she has continued this practice, and now her classroom runs very smoothly. So in my view, my ideas about being an outstanding teacher have rubbed off on her. In fact, we talk very often about teaching, and she keeps me motivated to want to continue teaching and inspiring young people to pursue teacher education.

CHAPTER 9
ADVICE TO PROSPECTIVE TEACHERS

I like to give advice to prospective and new teachers. That is because I think that I have knowledge and wisdom that can help them be successful in the classroom. Today I tell prospective teachers that they must learn how to *study*. Different people learn from different ways of using their senses. I think that students must determine how they learn best and apply these learning skills in college. No one tells you how to or when to study. You must learn what

works best for you … and learn it quickly. More specifically, I tell students that when they read a chapter, they should look at the headings of each section and turn those headings or statements into questions. As they read, they must keep the question (s) in mind, and when they complete reading that section, they need to determine if they can answer the question (s). If they can, then they understand what the section intended to teach them. They should continue to use this strategy among others until they complete the chapter.

I have also told prospective teachers that they should *visit the professor* as often as possible and ask the professor to explain concepts they do not understand. Professors love for students to visit them. It makes them feel special and important, and they want you as a student to learn. I have found that the students who visit their professors on a regular basis seem to perform better in the classroom. In addition, by visiting the professors, students get an opportunity to find out what they will encounter on tests. While the professors do not reveal the exact questions on upcoming examinations, they will tell the students about the topics that the students should know and be able to explain. This gives students an opportunity to better study and prepare for the tests.

I agreed with Halmos (1987) when he said that he advised students to never attend a graduate program at the same institution where they earned their undergraduate work. I was surprised when I read his work because I myself had said the same thing to students at the universities in which I worked. Attending different universities affords students a different perspective on learning, and it also exposes students to different cultures. More specifically, I tell students that going to a different university provides an opportunity for them to meet new people, to learn from a different culture, to gain new views, ideas, and knowledge, and to increase their span of networking with different cultures. I think each institution has its own culture, and students who are pursuing a graduate degree should get to know the institution so that they can understand the culture before they begin the graduate program. I say that because when I decided to go to graduate school, I applied to one university, got to know it very well, and talked to others in the graduate education program. I learned very quickly that I would not fit in very well at that institution with that culture, so when I looked at American University in Washington, DC, and talked to faculty members, administrators, and other students, I felt very comfortable and decided that I would fit in very well. In fact, the college of education must have wanted me because the dean of education enticed me with a full fellowship to study educational administration. I was pleased with the offer, and I attended and did very well. Now I can honestly say that I am proud to be a graduate of American University. In addition, I encourage students not to take life so serious. Today students must study, network, meet with their professors, and socialize. They should take time to have fun, such as playing golf, tennis, chess, scrabble, and go dancing, to name a few. They should also socialize by going to parties, cultural events, churches, and maybe pledge a sorority or fraternity. I think that these kinds of activities give students an opportunity to socialize with a diverse group of young people who are similar to them. Once they leave college, they will never again be surrounded by such a large group of like-minded people. The world of work, church, sorority, and other social groups will not be as diverse once they complete college and begin their careers.

While I think pre-service teachers must be highly motivated and must also love teaching, they need a little time for themselves to relax, reflex, and share with other prospective colleagues.

I also tell graduate students that when they decide to go to graduate school, they should choose a topic for their thesis or dissertation very early. This will give them an opportunity to focus on that topic throughout their entire course load, especially in their doctoral program. For example, when I enrolled in graduate school, I decided that my research work would focus on gifted education. In 1984, when I enrolled in graduate school, gifted education was a hot topic, and gifted education programs had just begun to pop up in school districts around the country. So I choose gifted education, and every paper that I wrote centered on some form of gifted education. When I took a course in administration that related to the budget, my papers focused on designing a budget for gifted education programs. When I took a course in curriculum, instruction, and assessment, my papers for the course focused on curriculum, instruction, and assessment of gifted education programs. You get the idea. I did the same thing for each course, and by the time I completed all of the courses and had to think specifically about what I was going to do with gifted education, I already had more than two hundred reference cards relating to gifted education that I could use for my dissertation. I think that this strategy made my dissertation process much easier.

As a young teacher, I never did get too involved in politics. Although I voted as a Democrat in each election, I really showed my support after retirement when I worked on the Obama campaign in 2008 and 2012. I wanted him to win so that I could proudly say that I had lived long enough to see a smart, wise, intelligent, funny, loving, and charismatic young African-American man in the White House of the United States. Those teachers who did not get to know him as president of the United States should read about him. He was one of the best presidents of the United States.

CHAPTER 10
HOW TO BE A
TEACHER

Wanting and becoming a teacher means that one should know what teachers need, what they should be able to do, and what they should care about to be able to perform effectively in the classroom. Everything I have said comes from my experience of being a teacher and learning about how to teach as I grew from a student to a scholar and then to a senior in retirement.

Teachers need to be well prepared and trained with a firm foundation in content as well as professional knowledge and skills. Teachers need to be well prepared so that when they step into the classroom with diverse students, other teachers, angry parents, and aggressive leaders cannot blow them away and criticize them for not knowing how to teach.

I have read the research on teacher education just to see if my opinion about being an effective teacher was correct. As I read, I found that I was not very far off in my thinking. I have gained a set of theoretical and methodological tools, not to mention a research literature background, all of which have helped me become an outstanding teacher. I believe that teachers must be successful in the classroom to help students learn. The research I reviewed showed that to be successful, teachers must be knowledge experts—that is, they must know the content that they are going to teach. If you are in a program that does not require you to take at least twelve hours of mathematics (geometry, number theory, algebra, problem solving, probability, statistics, and data analysis), ask yourself, "How am I going to best teach this generation of students when I do not have the background myself?" Teachers must also be learning experts—that is, they need to be experts in the field of education. While teachers may not be an expert at the undergraduate level, they should be well on their way to graduate school to learn as much as they can about teaching and learning. Personally, I continue to read and write in order to remain on the cutting edge in teacher education. Teachers must be critical thinkers too— that is, they have to always think about how to best help students learn. I am always thinking of new ways of helping students learn. Teachers need to be problem solvers, critical thinkers, and reflective practitioners as well. Obviously, effective teachers know how to solve the academic problems that students face. In fact, I think that I can solve an array of problems; however, I also realize that the administration above me may not always agree with the solutions. Finally, teachers must have excellent work ethics. I believe that teachers should facilitate learning and give the students an opportunity to shine without forcing their own views on the students (Schmidt, 2013). I did not know that William Schmidt also believed that teachers should possess these characteristics. I agree that teachers must have content knowledge, especially in the subjects of science, technology, engineering, and mathematics (STEM), pedagogical skills, and positive attitudes to be successful. They must know how to teach students so that those students can learn how to think critically, analytically, and solve everyday problems. They need other skills too, but when teachers know their content, understand how to help students learn, and notice when the students have mastered the material, they are much more successful in the classroom (Gilchrist, 2015). Along with these skills, teachers must also acknowledge the pressure coming from various societies that they must remain relevant and meaningful and understand academic concepts to function in a global society. This requires a new type of teaching force that must be proficient in the STEM subjects.

Teacher quality is one of the most important factors contributing to student achievement (Darling-Hammond, 2000). In order for future teachers to continue to be effective in the classroom, they must practice careful and adequate preparation (Cochran-Smith, 2004). Teacher preparation and development are critical dimensions in improving teacher quality and increasing student achievement (Darling-Hammond, 2000).

Effective teaching matters, and every child should have a good teacher (Obama, 2014; Duncan, 2014). Many school systems around the country believe that the teacher is the key to student success. In fact, the teacher is at the heart of success in student academics, and good teachers are the keys to closing the achievement gap (California State Department of Education, 2014). The research shows that students benefit from high-quality instruction, and good teachers are needed for student success (National Academy of Education, 2009).

Schmidt (2013) believed that good teachers must be competent in mathematics. In fact, he laid out a threefold approach to better preparing teachers of mathematics. He reported that (1) teachers with stronger mathematics background should be recruited to teach, (2) more rigorous state certification requirements should be implemented for mathematics teachers, and (3) more demanding mathematics courses for teacher preparation programs should be required. He also reported that future teachers need to have a broad base of knowledge in the theoretical and practical aspect of teaching mathematics and teaching in general.

We must move fast in restructuring teacher preparation programs. Schools and colleges of education need to rethink how teachers have been prepared in the past and look for new ways to prepare them to meet the demands of a changing society. In fact, schools and colleges of education need to rethink (1) how future teacher will be recruited; (2) what future teachers need to know and what they must be able to demonstrate; (3) how future teachers will be prepared, coached, mentored, and supported; (4) how to best pay quality teachers so that they remain in the classroom; and (5) how to provide ongoing professional development to keep teachers current (US Department of Education, 2013; Schneider, 2012).

The colleges and universities around the world that make up the National Institute of Education (NIE, 2008) believe that improvement in teacher quality requires a reconceptualization of how we should prepare this new generation of teachers. Their pathways for the preparation of teachers have a common thread. They want to maintain diversity in the field of teaching, and they also want to require continual innovation to develop a new generation of teachers. Moreover, they recommend a closer integration of academic knowledge, pedagogical skills, and teaching attitudes, and finally, they want to establish successful partnerships with governments, universities, and public schools. In fact, it seems that policy issues everywhere address (1) the recruitment and selection of good teachers and (2) the preparation and graduation of good teachers for the workforce (NIE, 2013). Everyone seems to agree that a high-quality teaching force is indispensable to the improvement of education quality (NIE, 2010). Regardless of the current educational system, all schools of education have to rethink their teacher preparation programs so that they can fit into the new global context.

Each educational system of the world is a function of its country's own unique historical, social, political, and cultural milieu (Gillespie, 2014). Nevertheless, there are certain factors that all teachers must know and be able to do to function in a global society. In fact, countries like China have already moved fast to train STEM leaders in order to help improve their teaching force. The Tans-Century Teacher Training Project called for the selection and training of a hundred thousand teachers to play key roles as instructional leaders, mentors, and specialists in research and pedagogy. Today teachers make up about 30 percent of the teaching force in China, according to the 2013 report out of the National Institute of Education (Gillespie, 2014).

Teachers needed a good understanding of (1) the content of core subjects, (2) global awareness, (3) financial, economic, and business literacy, (4) civic literacy, (5) health literacy, (6) environmental literacy, and (7) learning and innovation skills (AACTE, 2015). One research study asked teachers what they needed to be effective in the classroom, and the majority reported that they needed the following: (1) content and performance standards, (2) student assessment practices, (3) classroom management, (4) instructional practices, and (5) subject fields (AACTE, 2012). Teachers must be able to think critically, practice flexibility, and apply intercultural knowledge and awareness. The content knowledge must include science, technology, engineering, and mathematics (STEM). In short, all teachers in a global society must be proficient in the STEM subjects. If teachers are grounded in these core subjects, they will have a broad knowledge base to teach these subjects more effectively. In addition to the content knowledge, effective teachers need to know how to (1) communicate effectively with students, (2) motivate and inspire students to become lifelong learners, (3) manage complex ways of thinking, and (4) work effectively with their peers and colleagues (Scott, 2015). In other words, teaching is no longer curriculum-and teacher-centered. It is about student learning—that is, knowledge, skills, character, and learning.

Teachers need to know how to learn so that they can teach their students how to learn. They need to have the tools for working in diverse settings and classrooms. They need information and communication technology as well as information literacy. They need to possess skills for living, citizenship, career, and personal and social responsibility. Teacher must know various methods for teaching students how to think, how to work effectively, and how to develop life skills, and they must apply the tools of learning and working. Because of modernization, teachers must become lifelong learners, and they have to teach students to become life-long learners and manage complex ways of thinking and working. Teachers must know how to (1) embrace diversity with different pedagogical practices, (2) work with high-level knowledge and constantly advance their own professional knowledge, and (3) serve as agents of change and innovations (Teaching and Learning International Survey, 2013). In fact, teachers should be transfor-mational leaders. Teachers need to understand how children learn and grow. Although they may have taken a course in human de-velopment and educational psychology, this knowledge base may not have had a direct effect on teaching and learning. Research shows that teachers interpret new ideas through their past expe-riences and their established beliefs about teaching and learning (Pedagogy Inquiry-Based Teaching and Learning, 2012; National Institute for Educational Research, 2014; Garner-Gilchrist, 1996). Good teachers must know how to use the different pedagogical approaches and when to apply them. There is no perfect way of teaching; however, good teachers must have knowledge, skills, and dispositions so that they continue to be effective in the classroom (Fidel, 2013; Gilchrist, 1992). When expectations for teachers and students are raised to a higher standard, they rise to the challenge and produce at a higher level of achievement (Henderson, 2013; Scott, C., 2015). Therefore, teacher quality is very important to student learning and achievement (Graham, 2013).

Schools and colleges of education must continue to recruit the best students to become teachers. These schools and colleges have a responsibility to nurture, coach, mentor, and teach pro-spective teachers what they need in order to remain effective in the classroom. They must continue to select caring persons who are concerned about the whole child. Essentially, teachers must know the theories of learning and teaching as well as the practical application of learning and teaching.

As Paul Halmos (1987) said that he spent most of his life trying to be a great teacher and what did he learn? After reading his book, I began to think about what it takes to be a teacher. After my twenty years or more in the teaching profession, I am a believer that teaching is almost like becoming a minister. Ministers are called, which means that they have to have a passion for imparting the word of God to others. Well, teachers have to be born teachers—that is, one has to be born right (Halmos, 1985). A teacher has to be born with high intelligence. They have to have insight and vision. They must have patience, determination, a sense of humor, and love students. They must have sympathy and empathy for students. They have to be dedicated to the profession and communicate in a way that students understand, and they must have a style of teaching that helps students grasp the subjects. They also must have a warm and pleasing personality so that students will want to learn. They must have excellent planning skills, implementation strategies, and assessment approaches that do not scare students. They must know how to work well with other teachers, parents, and administrators. They must be responsible, conscientious, careful, and well organized (Halmos, 1985).

Teachers have to be as perfect as possible (Halmos, 1987). Teachers have to love the teaching profession and love students very much. They have to be morally responsible. They must love teaching more than anything else. That love must be powerful enough to keep them from giving up when they feel like quitting. Lots of people are teachers in some capacity, but do they love the teaching profession or the students? If certain people are going to be teachers, they must have the passion even before they go to college to obtain the degree and learn the theories. No one can teach another person how to love working with students. Teachers have to possess that trait long before they enter the classroom. If prospective teachers want to enter the teaching profession, they must look into their souls and determine how much they want to work with students (Halmos, 1987). When I first started working on my doctorate degree, the amount of work was overwhelming, and I initially thought that I could not do it; however, I knew I wanted that doctorate. So I searched my soul, and I thought to myself, *I want this degree very much*. Then I set out to accomplish my goal. So if you decided to study teaching because you thought that the teacher preparation programs were easy, you may complete the program, but you will never be happy and satisfied. You must choose teaching because you love it and love students and feel good when they learn a difficult concept. You will have doubts. You will feel discouraged, and you will undoubtedly want to quit at times. Outstanding teachers never quit because they love teaching students. They may need to take a break, go on vacation, and relax, but they will inevitably continue to teach and love students (Halmos, 1987). Teachers are human beings, and they have timely obligations and children of their own; however, even with all of the responsibilities, they must learn how to manage their personal lives and their teaching lives. They must set aside time to think and plan before they reach the students (Halmos, 1987). After I read Dr. Halmos' book *I Want to Be a Mathematician*, I concluded that he and I had experienced many of the same feelings and ideas about being a teacher. To be great teachers, they must love students and love teaching them. Teachers must be willing to work hard because it takes time to think, plan, implement, and assess lessons plans. If teachers do all of these things and the students still do not understand, teachers must do it over and over again, but in a different style until the students learn (Halmos, 1985).

Great teachers must plan ... and I mean plan well. They must know how to write objectives, how to assess what students already know, and how to use a variety of teaching strategies to meet the needs of diverse students in the classroom. I have always said that if teachers planned activities based on student learning styles, students will learn. For example, if teachers were teaching a lesson on geometric concepts, they could use concrete objects to help students understand the concepts. If they were teaching the concept of perimeter, they could have the student's measure the length and width of the room, and then they could talk about how long and how wide the room was. They could all compute the perimeter together. Then they could actually measure the length and width of a box to compute its perimeter. After they understood the concept, the students could measure the length and width of a box on paper to compute the perimeter. At the abstract level, the students could read a problem, then, talk about the length and width of the box and compute the perimeter. If students have had the experience of computing the perimeter in all three ways, they will likely understand perimeter, and hopefully they will be able to find the perimeter of any polygon. These are just examples to show prospective teachers how they can teach so that all students can learn. Some students are visual learners. Others learn well from hearing the information, and some can easily understand it from an abstract level.

I consider myself an expert teacher, especially in elementary and middle school mathematics. I have taught for more than thirty years, and I know that my students have learned and have been successful. I really cannot say for sure how teachers evolve and what they should become. I can only share what I did as a teacher.

As I was writing, I continued to keep my hands in teacher education. I was invited to travel to Liberia, West Africa, with the president of the National Association of University Women (NAUW) and her cabinet. While I was there, I conducted a workshop on teaching mathematics at the elementary school level. I was also invited to present at the 2014 American Middle School Convention and the 2014 Hawaii Convention on Education, and I also served as the 2015 keynote speaker at the Convention of the Higher Education Forum in Beijing, China, and at the 2015 International Conference on Social Science and Education in Tokyo, Japan. In each of these conventions, I focused on improving teacher quality and student achievement. I also tried to serve as a substitute teacher at the middle school level, and I found out that the students were not mathematical savvy. In addition to teaching whatever lessons the teachers had left—mostly work that bored the students—I taught mathematics, science, English, or social studies for the day. Some teachers even wrote me up for not making the students do the work that they had left for them.

As a seasoned educator, I knew that if I did not have exciting work for the students, they were going to talk, act out, and end up in the principal's office, and I did not want that to happen. I decided right away that substituting was not a good match for me. Soon I thought that I could become a full-time middle school teacher of mathematics, so I applied and found out that the state of South Carolina did not have reciprocity with the state of Virginia. Consequently, I had to take the Praxis II in order to teach. My teaching credentials in the state of Virginia remained current, but the South Carolina Department of Education had informed me that I had to become certified to teach in the state. Although I had been training teachers and teaching workshops on Praxis II, the South Carolina Department of Education would not certify me. I decided that I did not need to teach, so I continued to attend conferences and conventions on education. As of the writing of this book, I have been invited to present a scholarly paper on teacher quality at the 2015 International Conference on Education in Hong Kong and the 2016 International Conference on Education in Honolulu, Hawaii.

My travel certainly did influence how I taught in my later years because while I was in China, Japan, and Germany, I learned that students wanted to learn, and they put a lot of time and effort into studying. When I returned home, I decided that I needed to continue to help students understand why they needed to study and how to study correctly.

Well, what's next? Writing my book has been very trying. It took almost five years to complete it, but I could not finish it until I retired. I had been dreaming about writing a book for new teachers for a long time, but somehow I could not complete the project until now. I hope that you learned something from my experiences as a teacher, professor, consultant, and educator. I hope you are blessed in your new position as a teacher. I have always wanted to be a teacher. I was a teacher, and now that I am retired, I still want to be a teacher. And who knows? I may return to the workforce one day. It is in my blood. I cannot help it; I want to be a teacher.

EPILOGUE

After I completed this book, I decided to return to the workforce. You see, I still want to be a teacher. After I retired, I was not satisfied because teaching was in my blood. It was a part of me. I thought that I had more to offer prospective teachers. I became the chairperson of the division of education at Morris College in Sumter, South Carolina. The chair of the division of education is similar to a dean of education, a position I had also held in three previous universities. The major difference was that at Morris College, the chairs taught nine semester hours in addition to serving as the chair. I enjoyed this approach because it required that I remain on the cutting edge of the developments of teacher education.

When I returned to the workforce, I taught a course in elementary and middle school mathematics, which focused on algebra, geometry, number theory, probability, statistics, data analysis, and problem solving. This was excellent for me because I had always liked mathematics. You see, I have always believed that prospective teachers should pursue at least twelve hours of mathematics in order to be effective in the classroom. In short, I still want to teach, and that is something I learned.

I am enjoying my position at Morris College as the chairperson of the division of education. We are on a fast track to accomplish all that needs to be done to undergo the reaffirmation of the accreditation of the teacher preparation program.

ABOUT THE AUTHOR

Dr. Scott is a leading scholar in the field of teacher preparation of higher education. Her article on the need for a paradigm shift in teacher preparation for schools of education appears in the spring 2013 issue of the *Journal of the National Association of University Women*, and she has offered her expertise on this issue at the local, national, and international levels. In addition, Dr. Scott is a prominent educator whose distinctive career has been marked by a host of positions in leadership, education, training, and development. She has been the dean and professor of education at Claflin University, Orangeburg, South Carolina and Cheyney University, Cheyney, Pennsylvania; assistant and associate dean of education and director of teacher education at North Carolina Central University, Durham, North Carolina and Benedict College, Columbia, South Carolina; professor of education at Hampton University, Hampton, Virginia; a summer education research fellow at the National Aeronautical and Space Administration (NASA), Langley, Virginia;

a public school teacher in the school districts of the District of Columbia, and Prince George's and Ann Arundel Counties, Maryland, and the US Department of Defense Schools in Germany. Dr. Scott has presented numerous papers and workshops at international, national, regional, state, and local conferences and conventions on improving teacher quality, student achievement, and leadership skills. Her most recent presentations were at the 2015 International Symposium on Social Science and Management in Tokyo, Japan and the 2014 International Conference on Higher Education in Beijing, China, where she served as the Keynote Speaker on Teacher Quality and Student Achievement.

Dr. Scott has had intensive preparation and study. She holds a Doctor of Philosophy Degree (Ph.D.) in Leadership, Education, Training and Development from the American University, Washington, DC, and a Master's Degree in Elementary School Mathematics from the University of Maryland, College Park, Maryland, and a Bachelor of Arts Degree in Early Childhood and Elementary Education from Norfolk State University, Norfolk, Virginia. She has completed further study in education at Bowie State College, Bowie, Maryland, and Howard University and Trinity College, Washington, DC. In addition, she has completed advance leadership studies through the Bryn Mawr University Summer Leadership Institute for Women, Bryn Mawr, Pennsylvania, the Hampton University Presidential Leadership Institute, and the Commonwealth of Pennsylvania Executive Leadership Institute.

Dr. Scott has served public and private education very well. Based on her proposal writing ability, skills, and dedication to education, she was very instrumental in securing funds over five million dollars from the National Aeronautics and Space Administration, the Virginia State Department of Education, the Virginia Commission on Higher Education, the United States Department of Human Services, the United States Department of Education, the Pennsylvania Department of Education, and the Tom Joyner Foundation, to train and develop pre-service and in-service teachers in mathematics and science.

Dr. Scott authored and was involved in numerous professional publications focusing on the improvement of teaching and learning for elementary and middle school students and teachers. These publications came as a result of research conducted from Mathematics Summer Institutes for Elementary and Middle School Students and Teachers. She has served as a grant reader on education for the United States Department of Human Services, the United States Department of Education, the Virginia State Department of Education, North Carolina State Department of Education, and the Pennsylvania State Department of Education.

Dr. Scott holds membership in numerous civic organizations and religious affiliations, such as the Board of Directors of the Young Women Christian Association, the National Coalition of 100 Black Women, the National Association of Negro Women, the National Association of University Women, the American Association of University Women, the American Educational Research Association, Alpha Kappa Alpha Sorority and the Order of Eastern Star. She has been involved in her community as a Church Deaconess, Director of Christian Education, Sunday School Teacher, Missionary, Usher Board, and Choir at the Antioch Baptist Church, Washington, DC, Usher and Choir Member and Sunday School Teacher at the Diamond Grove Baptist Church, Skippers, Virginia; and Director of Christian Education, Vacation Bible School, Children's Programs at the Frankfurt, Germany Military Base. She has always been involved in her church and community activities. She is a member of the International Bible Study Fellowship Program in Columbia, South Carolina and currently a member of the Antioch AME Zion Church, Eastover, South Carolina.

Dr. Scott has received awards and certificates of appreciation from numerous organizations, such as the National Association of University Women, the National Council of Negro Women, Alpha Kappa Alpha Sorority, and Boys and Girls Clubs of America. Dr. Scott is a world traveler to all of the continents, except Antarctica and Australia. In North America, she traveled throughout the

United States to include the islands of Hawaii, Puerto Rico, St. Thomas, Aruba, Nassau, Mexico, Trinidad, Barbados, and Canada. In South America, she traveled to the countries of Brazil and Panama. In Europe, she traveled to Germany, Holland, Italy, and France. In Asia, she traveled to Japan and China, and in Africa, she traveled to South Africa, Swaziland, Ghana, and Liberia.

Dr. Scott is highly motivated and motivates others to rethink old ways of doing business. She views challenges and problems from a different perspective and seeks creative solutions to problems. She views herself as a visionary and transformational leader who is highly motivated, professional, determined, and energetic. She is committed to high quality service and education.

Dr. Scott serves as a role model to young women and girls for her wisdom, strength, courage, dignity, beauty, and resiliency. She is currently the Founder and President of the National Young Minority Girls Academy, a non-profit organization, designed to serve as a voice to improve the education and leadership skills of young girls in grades four through six. She is also the Vice President and Chief Executive Officer for Research, Education, Training and Development of G & H Educational and Research Foundation, Inc., a consulting firm in South Carolina. Her story is exemplary because she represents a model of excellence for young people today and tomorrow, and she continues to instill in young women and girls the need to remain life-long learners and to get in and remain in the habit of saving money.

More than ten people read every word of this book. Their comments either made me angry or made me happy, but in either case, their comments spurred me on. They are Gertrude Henry (long-time colleague), Louvenia Magee Richards (long-time personal friend), Edward Garner, Jr. (brother), Gretchen Cathine Gilchrist, Glenda Cathine Pinkett, Giena Cathine Gilchrist (daughters), Dorothy Kornegay (first cousin), Loretta Johnson Butts (long-time college friend), and Robert L. Scott (husband). Thanks a million!

BIBLIOGRAPHY

Allen, D. C. (2015). Learning auto-ethnography: a review of auto-ethnography: The Qualitative Report (20). No.2.33-35. Retrieved from the http://www/nov.wdu/ssss.

Ames. C. A. (2013). "What teachers need to know?" Teachers College Board. Volume 91. November 3 spring, 1990. Teachers College, Columbia University.

American Association of Colleges and Teacher Education (2010). Twenty-first Century knowledge and skills in education preparation. Washington, DC.

Askew, J. (2014). "What is a successful teacher?" Retrieved from the Internet.

Bybee, J. (2013). "Improving teacher and principal quality." California State Department of Education Education. Retrieved from the internet at www.cde.ca.gov.

Chang, H. (2008). *Auto-ethnography: A Method.* Walnut Creek, CA: Left Coast.

Cochran-Smith, M. (2005). "Studying teacher education": The report of the American Education Research Association. Mahwah, New Jersey.

Darling-Hammond, L. (2011). *The flat world and education: How America's commitment to equity will determine our future.* New York: Teacher College Press.

Duncan, A. (2014). "Educating our children." Speech at Allen University, Columbia, SC.

Ellis, C., T. Adams, and A. Bochner (2010). "Auto-ethnography: An Overview." *Forum: Qualitative Social Research* 12.

Ellis, C., and A. Bochner (2000). "Auto-ethnography: Personal narrative and reflexivity." In N. K. Denzinty & Lincoln's, eds., *Handbook of Qualitative Research.* Thousands Oaks, CA: Sage.

Gilchrist-Scott (2012). "Improving teacher quality and increasing student achievement." Presentation at the American Middle Level Education Association.

Gillespie, N. (2015). "Creating a national network of STEM teacher leaders." *Education Week* 33, no. 2.

Gopinathan, S. S., Tan, and Yanping, F. (2010). "Transforming teacher education". Redefined professionals for the twenty-first century schools. National Institute of Education. Singapore Nanyan Technological University.

Halmos, P. (1987). *I want to be a mathematician: An automathography in three parts.* Mathematical Association of America, Inc: Washington, DC.

Harris, D. and Sass, T. (2008). "Teacher training, teacher quality, and student achievement." National Center for Analysis of Longitudinal Data in Education Research: The Urban Institute.

Joyce Foundation (2013). "Improving teacher quality." Retrieved from the Internet at www.joycefdn.org/teacher.

Lieberman, A., and Mace, D. (2010). "Making practice public: Teacher learning in the 21st century." *Journal of Teacher Education.*

Levine, A.(2014). "Educating school teachers". Retrieved from the Internet at http:www.edschools.org.

McDiarmid, B. and Salcito, A. (2013). "How to best prepare teachers for the future." Retrieved from the Internet.

National Academy of Education (2013). "Improving teacher quality and distribution." Washington, DC.

National Council for Accreditation of Teacher Education. (2011). "Transforming teacher education through clinical experiences: A national strategy to prepare effective teachers." Washington, DC. Retrieved from the Internet at www.ncate.org.

National Council on Teacher Quality (2011). "Student teaching in the United States". Retrieved from the Internet at www.nctq./org/student teaching.

National Research Council (2010). *"Preparing teachers: Building evidence for sound policy"*. Washington, DC: National Academy of Press.

Schmidt. W. (2013). "U.S. needs better-trained mathematics teachers." Retrieved from the Internet at http:usteds.msu.edu.

Schleicher, A. (2012). "Preparing teachers and developing leaders for the twenty-first century: Lessons from the world." Retrieved from www.**usatoday**.com/news/edu.

Varona, J. (2013). "An auto-mathography". Retrieved from www. math.umb.edu.

Wall, S. (2006). "An auto-ethnography on learning about auto-ethnography." *International Journal of Qualitative Methods* 5, no. 2.

Wall, S. (2008). "Easier said than done: Writing an auto-ethnography." *International Journal of Qualitative Methods* 17, no. 1

US Department of Education. (2014). "Our future, our teachers: The Obama administration's plan for teacher education reform and improvement." Retrieved from the Internet at http://www.2ed.gov/ln.

CPSIA information can be obtained
at www.ICGtesting.com
Printed in the USA
FFOW03n2217300617
37347FF

9 781480 826236